Wounded in the House of My Friends
By
Pastor Derek Craig Jones

2

Chapter list;

1: Wounded in the house of My friends. Page 5

2: When people are hurt. Page 32

3: Skandal. Page 57

4: When leaders fail. Page 77

5: Trust the Lord with Judgment. Page 97

6: Imagination, is it your friend or foe? Page 128

7: Bringing healing to the body. Page 153

Chapter 1: Wounded in the House of My Friends

Imagine this scene; **all of fallen humanity has assembled before God.** <u>It is Judgment Day!</u>

Their guilt is unquestioned, but they have a plan.

As God prepares to pass judgment on them they cry out, *"Unfair! We deserve to be judged by one of our own! We need someone who knows what it is to be human!"*

"Fair enough" said God, *"What would you like him to be like? Describe him to Me."*

"He needs to come from a questionable background!" shouted some.

Others said, *"He should be raised in a home where he has a step-parent so that he knows how it feels!"*

"Make him an outcast! Make it to where people treat him so bad that it is shameful!" other people demanded.

"Yes, and make him suffer terrible pain!"

"And You must turn Your back to him so that he understands what we feel when we sin!"

Finally someone spoke up and said, *"Make him a good man that nobody understands. Make it so that even his family thinks that he's crazy. Make his friends turn against him and desert him. Then he will be able to judge us!"*

All of the people shouted out their approval, thinking that God would be unable to meet their demands.

But God merely pointed to the empty cross and said, ***"That is exactly what I did, and you rejected and crucified Him! He is My Son and He will be your judge."***

Staring in shock at the empty cross they realized too late that God had already given them the fairest Judge and they rejected Him.

It was abundantly clear that God not only cared for them, He lived among them and suffered just like they did. He became one of them; lived, loved and abode with them, ***and they killed Him for it!***

The assembled crowd knew that it had nothing that it could say, each person there was guilty, and the Lord Jesus could judge them because He had lived among them. Dejectedly they bowed their heads and accepted His judgment.

Mankind always wants to think that God doesn't understand what they are going through, but He does. Everyone seems to think that they are so unique in their suffering that nobody else has ever felt their pain. But the truth is none of us suffer anything so unique that God can't comprehend it.

Through His Son Jesus Christ He experienced every pain and heartache known to man, even separation.

And His Son bears the marks on His body of His time around people!

He knows! He knows how you feel when people stomp on you!

He knows how it feels to be rejected, lied about, gossiped about, mocked and ridiculed.

He knows.

One day Jesus will return to this earth and He will still bear the marks of His crucifixion and suffering on His glorified body so that all mankind will understand that He knows!

"And one shall say to him, What are these wounds in your hands? Then he shall answer, ***Those with which I was wounded in the house of My friends."*** Zechariah 13:6

This passage describes the magnificent scene in Israel when the Lord Jesus returns at the Battle of Armageddon.

Israel will have been nearly annihilated by the armies of the antichrist. All hope for her survival will have been extinguished.

And then suddenly Jesus splits the Eastern Sky!

Their long awaited Messiah has come, just as they always pictured He would!

Riding on a magnificent white horse Jesus comes to their rescue as the armies of heaven follow Him, all of them riding white horses.

It is the most incredible spectacle in history! Television cameras will capture every angle and every picture as the Messiah of Israel sets His feet upon the Mount of Olives and rescues the nation of Israel.

But in the aftermath of the battle, when all enemies are vanquished, they notice something about the Messiah—**He has nail-prints in His hands and feet!**

The shock hits them all at once as they realize that their Messiah was Jesus Christ!

"How did You get those wounds in Your hands?" they ask through tears.

"I got these in the house of My friends" Jesus answers.

It will be the most shocking moment in the history of Israel when they finally realize the truth; their Messiah came to deliver them—and they crucified Him!

The joy of being delivered from total destruction will quickly give way to mourning as they realize the truth. For 20 Centuries they have wandered as vagabonds in the earth because they killed their King.

Everything that they suffered—*the holocaust and persecutions and anti-Semitism*—were all preventable! If they had only accepted Him when He came how different their history would have been!

That day the grief will sweep the remaining Israelites and their hearts will break when they realize what their ancestors did to their Messiah.

"And I will pour out on the house of David and the inhabitants of Jerusalem a spirit of grace and pleas for mercy, so that, when they look on me, on him whom they have pierced, they shall mourn for him, as one mourns for an only child, and weep bitterly over him, as one weeps over a firstborn" Zechariah 12:10

Jesus was wounded in the house of His friends!

The original Hebrew word translated *"friends"* is ***"aw-hab."*** And the literal translation of that word is "***those who love Me!***"

Jesus *"friends"* beat Him, spit upon His face and struck His head with a rod. Do you understand what this was like? He had to watch them—His creation—as they took turns hitting Him with the rod and spitting upon His face.

They slapped Him repeatedly. It jerked His head around each and every time.

And yet He gave them His cheeks to slap again and again.

He did not cower on the floor and beg for mercy! He stuck His chin out and waited on the next person to have their turn slapping His face as hard as they could.

They pulled out His beard! Not content to just humiliate Jesus by beating and spitting on Him they wanted to make Him unmanly by taking off His beard. Every Jew had a beard, so they were really trying to make Jesus appear as something less—***an excommunicated Jew.***

Yet He made no sound.

He just let them have their way with Him.

Somewhere in this melee Peter snuck into the courtyard and watched from a safe distance as they abused his Lord.

It was then that Jesus turned His face away from His tormentors and looked Peter squarely in the eyes!

It was as if a conversation happened all by one look!

Peter had just denied for the third time that he even knew who Jesus; and then the Lord looked at him!

Instead of rising up and defending Jesus, Peter ran off and wept bitterly. His time of making a difference passed him by that day, but fortunately Jesus would give him another chance.

But he could have come and stood by Jesus that day! He clearly wanted to, but fear stopped him. Just like fear stops many Christians from defending Jesus to their friends and neighbors.

Then they delivered Him to the Romans to be killed.

His *"friends"* the Jews watched and approved of Him being beaten half to death with a cat-o-nine tails whip.

They jeered and ridiculed Him as He walked to Calvary to be crucified.

And then they stood at the foot of His cross and made fun of Him as He hung there dying for their sins!

With *"friends"* like those who needs enemies!?

Those *"friends"* enjoyed seeing Jesus bleed!

They were actually happy when they saw the results of the cat-o-nine tails!

His swollen face that had been repeatedly struck only served to embolden them to ridicule Him even more.

They showed Him no sympathy at all!

The Psalmist David wrote about this very day hundreds of years before it happened. In **Psalm 22** he expresses the suffering of Jesus as He looks down from the cross;

"But I am a worm and not a man, scorned by mankind and despised by the people. All who see me mock me; they make mouths at me; they wag their heads; "He trusts in the LORD; let him deliver him; let him rescue him, for he delights in him!" Psalm 22:6-8

Scorned, and despised! No pity. No mercy. No love.

The Savior received from the people nothing but hatred.

A devilish jealousy fueled the priests to act as they did. Many others were just too afraid to have anyone accuse them of being a Jesus sympathizer, so they went along with the crowd.

God's Word told exactly what was going to happen to the Son of God centuries before it happened. Israel was unwittingly fulfilling the prophecies by their treatment of Jesus Christ.

"He had no form or majesty that we should look at him, and no beauty that we should desire him. He was despised and rejected by men; a man of sorrows, and acquainted with grief; and as one from whom men hide their faces he was despised, and we esteemed him not. Surely he has borne our griefs and carried our sorrows; yet we esteemed him stricken, smitten by God, and afflicted. But he was pierced for our transgressions; he was crushed for our iniquities; upon him was the chastisement that brought us peace, and with his wounds we are healed." Isaiah 53:2-5

A man of sorrows—acquainted with grief!

He was WELL-ACQUAINTED with grief!

Three times in the Gospel records the Lord Jesus wept. Once for the hurting of a family who had lost a loved one, (John 11: 1-45)

Once He wept over Jerusalem as He described in detail its coming destruction (Luke 19:41-44)

And He wept very strongly in the Garden of Gethsemane as He prayed for there to be another way instead of the way of the cross. (Hebrews 5:7)

There can be little doubt that He wept at other times also.

He was no stranger to our pain! He felt excluded at times, insulted, ridiculed, mocked, they questioned his lineage and who His Father was, and they constantly watched Him in order to condemn Him.

Most of us would have ended up becoming nervous wrecks if we had to endure the attacks upon our character that Jesus was forced to endure each and every day.

Israel punished their Savior so terribly that He would be excused if He decided to NOT save them!

Who could blame the Lord Jesus if He said that we were too rotten to save?

His blood was so pure and our sins so awful that we did not deserve one drop of it.

Yet He not only endured suffering and shame, He embraced it and owned it and triumphed over it.

Although it had been written in their sacred texts, Israel never dreamed it applied to the Messiah.

Luke records that it happened exactly as David had prophesied;

"The rulers scoffed at him, saying, "He saved others; let him save himself, if he is the Christ of God, his Chosen One!" The soldiers also mocked him, coming up and offering him sour wine and saying, "If you are the King of the Jews, save yourself!" Luke 23:35-37

Do you realize how POWERFUL that Jesus was?

He COULD HAVE called 12 legions of warrior angels down and they would have annihilated His enemies in an instant!

He could have easily proven to His skeptics that He was truly the Son of God by stepping off of the cross.

He could have—but He didn't!

He chose to undergo such torment and affliction to pay the price for sinners like me.

If He had given in and stepped away from the punishment of the cross I would have been forever lost!

So He stayed there and let them keep piling on the insults and the abuse.

By the time that Jesus made it to the cross He had already been awake for over 24 hours and had endured unspeakable abuse.

He had to have been so exhausted and physically weak that without God's help He couldn't have made the journey up Calvary's hill.

But His misery was far from over, as He was about to endure much worse suffering and mocking.

Mark tells us that the crowd was mocking Him also;

And those who passed by derided him, wagging their heads and saying, "Aha! You who would destroy the temple and rebuild it in three days, save yourself, and come down from the cross!" Mark 15:29-30

They had no pity on the Creator when they could have.

They showed no remorse for the fact that they knew that He was innocent; they knew that He came from God and they knew that they were sinning by condemning Him.

His gentle touch had healed them of their diseases and yet they nailed those hands to the cross!

His voice had commanded demons to leave the people that they had possessed and now they mock His words!

His calloused feet traveled many miles to bring the Good News to them and to give deliverance to them and their families, and now they have nailed them to the cross!

Had they no conscience?

Didn't they remember any of the good things that Jesus had done for them?

I want to say to you that those Jews were absolutely no different than people today.

Jesus' *"friends"* claimed to love God, but their hearts were so hardened by religion and sin that they didn't even recognize Him when He stood before them.

Their hearts were evil. Every thought of their wicked hearts were selfish. Even though the Lord performed mighty miracles and healed thousands of them, they turned against Him.

As the Lord Jesus said to them, *"Well did Isaiah prophesy of you, when he said: "This people honors me with their lips, but their heart is far from me"* Matthew 15:7-8

There is probably no hurt as deep as when a loved one turns against you.

The thing about Jesus though was that He knew it was coming, so He didn't expect any differently.

He often spoke of the people's false love for God;

"Indeed, in their case the prophecy of Isaiah is fulfilled that says: "You will indeed hear but never understand, and you will indeed see but never perceive." For this people's heart has grown dull, and with their ears they can barely hear, and their eyes they have closed, lest they should see with their eyes and hear with their ears and understand with their heart and turn, and I would heal them." Matthew 13:15

This was not a new thing in Israel just as it is not a new thing in America or anywhere else. False worship that does not require the heart is prevalent.

Hundreds of years before Christ was born the prophet Ezekiel dealt with the same type of people;

"And they come unto you as the people come, and they sit before you as my people, and they hear your words, but they will not do them: for with their mouth they show much love, but their heart goes after their covetousness." Ezekiel 33:31.

Heart worship is required to serve God. He will not accept empty words.

The people in front of Ezekiel thought that they were alright, but the God they mocked could see into their hearts and He was very displeased with what He saw there.

Faithless friends. Bitter enemies. False friends. The wrong side seeming to win. Ridiculed, mocked, beaten, lied on, humiliated and shamed. Jesus endured it all and more for your sake and mine.

If we were to turn from the angry crowd standing there jeering at our Savior we would see interspersed among them sorrowful faces.

They are the faces of Jesus' mother Mary, her sister and some friends along with one of His disciples—John.

There were no doubt others standing nearby who had been healed by the Savior. He healed so many thousands that it is inconceivable that none of them were there that day.

He had healed them, and now they watched Him suffer and die!

Put yourself into the shoes of one of those people for a minute.

<u>Perhaps you were blind.</u> You had never seen a flower or a face or the sunshine. People described your world to you but you couldn't begin to picture it because you had no frame of reference to draw on.

All that you had ever seen was black. All you had ever dreamt of was black. It was your reality.

And then one day you heard that the prophet Jesus of Nazareth was coming your way!

Nervously you got up and went toward the sound of the crowd shouting out His name in the hope that He might heal you.

Amazingly Jesus did hear your cry!

"What is it that you desire from Me?" He asked.

"Lord, that I might see!" you replied.

Reaching out He placed His hands over your eyes and says simply, *"Be healed!"*

And suddenly you could see!

You would have just about worn your eyes out looking at everything those first few days!

But the first sight you saw was the Savior's face.

That same face that you saw that day is hanging on the cross.

Except that now His face is marred by beatings.

His beard has been ripped out in places.

Those eyes that looked deep into yours the day that He healed you are now nearly swollen shut from the beatings that He has endured.

Those hands that covered your eyes have nails piercing through them.

That mouth that spoke healing and light into your life is now swollen and bloody.

His few words that He speaks are sad and pitiful.

He shocks you by crying out, *"My God! My God! Why have You forsaken Me?"*

How would you feel standing there watching Him?

How would you look at your world after letting Jesus down?

There was one chance in your life to do something for the One who had healed you and given you back your life—and you refused to get involved.

How much do you value your eyesight now? The eyesight that Jesus gave you? Could you close your eyes and sleep after that?

I wonder; if you were the blind man and you watched the Lord suffer and die how would you react?

When the centurion shouted out, *"Surely this was a righteous man!"* would you have nodded your head in agreement?

After the suffering and agony was complete and they took Jesus down from the cross you would have headed home.

Sitting down to eat you would have looked upon the Passover meal of lamb, unleavened bread and bitter herbs.

For your whole life you have eaten Passover without ever seeing it, but this night you can see it, thanks to Jesus.

Later in the evening after reciting the Passover story of Moses and the deliverance of the children of Israel it is time to go to sleep. Would you have hesitated a moment as you contemplate blowing out the candle? Would you have laid down and stared into the pitch black of night and thought of how it used to be all that you could see or imagine.

And what is more, would your mind recall over and over again the agony of the Man called Jesus that you watched with eyes that He had touched and healed?

How could you deal with that?

But there were others who should have been there that day who owed everything to Jesus Christ.

There were many people that Jesus had helped, healed, delivered and even fed. So many thousands who owed Him their lives. Where were they at?

Do you remember the story of Simon the Leper?

He was a well-to do man, probably a Pharisee who had contracted the dread disease leprosy. In the Gospels we read that Simon gave a dinner and invited Jesus and His disciples.

This tells us that although he was known as Simon the leper he had to have been cured by Jesus. Otherwise he would never have been allowed by law to associate with anyone else except other lepers.

So obviously **he had been** a leper, and Jesus had cured him of that terrible disease.

Wouldn't you be thankful if that was you?

Leprosy was death to anyone who contracted it. It is a disease that eats away your hands, feet and face until your bones are exposed. To have leprosy was to have a death sentence. And Jesus took pity on Simon and healed him!

What did Simon do to repay that kindness? He invited Jesus to dinner, but notice how he acts.

*"And behold, a woman of the city, who was a sinner, when she learned that he was reclining at table in the Pharisee's house, brought an alabaster flask of ointment, and standing behind him at his feet, weeping, she began to wet his feet with her tears and wiped them with the hair of her head and kissed his feet and anointed them with the ointment. Now when the Pharisee who had invited him saw this, he said to himself, "**If this man were a prophet**, he would have known who and what sort of woman this is who is touching him, for she is a sinner." Luke 7:37-39*

"*If*" this Man were a prophet?!

He just healed you of leprosy!

You are only sitting here because of Jesus!

How ignorant and uncaring can one person be?

Jesus immediately discerned the thoughts of Simon and spoke to him about it. Looking at Simon He said to him *"Simon, I have something to say to you."*

Somewhat shocked into reality, Simon left his thoughts and answered the Lord, *"Say it, Teacher."*

<u>Jesus looked into Simon's eyes and spoke slowly</u>, *"A certain moneylender had two debtors. One owed five hundred denarii, and the other fifty. When they could not pay, he cancelled the debt of both.* **Now which of them will love him more?"** *Simon answered, "The one, I suppose, for whom he cancelled the larger debt." And Jesus said to him, "You have judged rightly."* <u>Luke 7:40-43</u>

Yes, he judged correctly, but he didn't really get it. So the Lord made it clear to him.

"Do you see this woman? I entered your house; you gave me no water for my feet, but she has wet my feet with her tears and wiped them with her hair. You gave me no kiss, but from the time I came in she has not ceased to kiss my feet. You did not anoint my head with oil, but she has anointed my feet with ointment. Therefore I tell you, her sins, which are many, are forgiven—for she loved much. But he who is forgiven little, loves little." <u>Luke 7:44-47</u>

It is clear that Simon felt that he deserved and had a right to judge others because of his status as a Pharisee.

Even though Jesus had healed him—delivering him from certain death!—he thought that he was on a higher plane than Christ.

He never referred to Jesus as Lord.

He never even called Him Rabbi.

He called Him *"didaskalos"* which means *"teacher."*

"Kurios" means Lord and that was what most people called Jesus.

"Rabboni" was the name that Mary Magdalene called Jesus and it meant *"Master teacher."*

Simon could have at least called Jesus Rabboni.

But Simon never thought highly enough of Jesus to give Him an exalted name or title. To Simon, Jesus' credentials were not impressive enough EVEN THOUGH HE WAS THE ONLY PERSON IN THE WORLD WHO COULD HEAL LEPROSY!

Where was Simon when Jesus needed a friend?

Bethany was a short walk from Calvary's cross. It is probable that Simon was either in the crowd that day or he knew what was going on.

Shouldn't he have at the very least stood there and told the authorities—who were probably his friends—that Jesus had healed him?

Surely he could testify of being saved from death!

But Simon was nowhere to be found that day. If he was in the crowd he made sure that he didn't stand apart from it.

How could you live with yourself after knowing that Jesus had saved your life and had given you back your life and you did nothing to save His?

What about the lame man that John tells us about in John 5:1-17?

John says that he had been an invalid for 38 years and that the Lord obviously took pity on him and healed him.

Was he thankful? Would you have been?

Because the Lord healed him on the Sabbath the man got into trouble for carrying his pallet on the holy day. If you or I had been an invalid for 38 years I doubt that we would care what day of the week we got our healing!

If the man called Jesus healed me and told me to skip all the way home I would do it!

The formerly lame man went walking down the main boulevard carrying his cot. This was expressly forbidden by Jewish Ceremonial Law. It wasn't anything that you would find in the Books of Moses, but they went beyond Moses and the bible when it came to rules and regulations. And a person could be stoned to death for breaking their ceremonial rules.

Seeing him walking home so happy carrying his cot infuriated the scribes and Pharisees and they immediately accosted the man and demanded to know why he was breaking the law. So he told them that a man had healed him and delivered him from being an invalid.

Instead of praising God they demanded to know who it was so they could straighten Him out. But the man didn't know who Jesus was so he couldn't tell them.

Later on Jesus saw Him in the Temple and said to him, *"See, you are well! Sin no more, that nothing worse may happen to you."* John 5:14.

How would you have reacted on meeting Jesus after He had delivered you from 38 years of being paralyzed?

Would you have fell at His feet and worshipped Him?

Wouldn't you at least have the decency to thank Him and want to do something for Him?

Not this man! He turned around and went to the Pharisees and told them it was Jesus who had healed him on the Sabbath!

That caused the religious authorities to persecute Jesus for breaking one of their rules. It wasn't God's rule, it was theirs.

But what about that man? Didn't he walk home after informing on Jesus? What was he thinking as he walked across the threshold of his home?

He lived in Jerusalem where Jesus was put on trial and crucified; surely he got up that morning and heard the noise!

Wouldn't you have at least walked out to see what all of the commotion was about?

Picture him walking towards the Temple complex; he sees a large and noisy crowd shouting out, **"Crucify Him! Crucify Him!"**

Wondering who it is that they are wanting to kill he presses through the crowd and sees a heart-wrenching sight!

It is Jesus. The one who healed him.

As he stands there I wonder if he looked down at his legs and feet?

There on the platform next to Pilate the Roman governor stands the man who gave him back his life! And He is about to be crucified.

Shouldn't he do something?

If he stood there that day he did nothing to help the Lord. He apparently just walked back home.

As he lay down that night I wonder if he felt ashamed of himself?

This was Jesus! He healed him from being a hopeless invalid. Nobody else ever did anything for him like that; shouldn't he have spoken up for Jesus even if the crowd was against him?

He let his fear get in the way of what was right.

But there were many other people there that day who failed the Lord in His greatest hour of need.

As the Lord Jesus surveyed the crowd that day I wonder how many of the people He recognized? How many of them had He healed? How many had come to Jesus for a miracle and had received it?

The Lord suffered terribly on the cross in the physical, but He also suffered terribly in the Spiritual.

When the sun withdrew its shining and the sky became black as night the sin of the whole world was placed upon Jesus our sacrifice.

God withdrew His presence from His Son and Jesus had to endure separation from His Father for the first and only time in history.

Grief-stricken He cried out, *"Eloi, Eloi, lema sabachthani?" which means "My God, My God! Why have You forsaken Me?"* Mark 15:34.

But Jesus' temptations were not confined to His last two days on earth. He had endured manifold temptations so that He could sympathize and understand mankind.

The writer of the book of Hebrews was dealing with people who were tempted to deny Jesus Christ was their Savior. They had come out of Judaism and were willing to go back if it would save them from persecution.

They felt alone against a hostile world.

They just wanted to live in peace.

That is understandable—to a point.

But there was a big problem; if they denied Jesus there was no one else who could save them.

Also there was no other Savior who could sympathize with them in their fears, weaknesses and temptations.

"For we do not have a high priest who is unable to sympathize with our weaknesses, but one who in every respect has been tempted as we are, yet without sin." Hebrews 4:15.

In other words, if you deny Jesus there is nobody left who can save you AND understand AND sympathize with you in your struggles because He has endured every temptation in every respect the same as you!

Every respect?! Was He really tempted with what you and I are tempted with? The answer is yes, exactly the same temptations because He faced exactly the same devil.

So it was tempting for Jesus to take revenge on people who lied about Him, ridiculed Him and insulted Him. It was a temptation. A temptation is something that you at least want or else it isn't even tempting.

Jesus must have been at least a little tempted by the thought of settling down and having a wife and children.

The things you deal with He dealt with!

But what about growing up? What about being rejected in His hometown of Nazareth? What about His brothers rejecting Him and worse? Didn't that ever bother Him?

If He was tempted in EVERY RESPECT just like us then, yes, it bothered Him!

He understood the temptation to avenge Himself.

"Therefore he had to be made like his brothers in every respect, so that he might become a merciful and faithful high priest in the service of God, to make propitiation for the sins of the people. For because he himself has suffered when tempted, he is able to help those who are being tempted." Hebrews 2:17-18

He had to know heartbreak and loss to understand what it does to us!

He had to know rejection.

He had to have really loved people and then had them turn against Him.

Friends who only love you for what they can get out of you are not true friends. They soon realize that you cannot do for them what they desire so they turn against you.

The Word of God declares that *"A friend loves at all times!"* Proverbs 17:17.

Those people were never really friends with Jesus. They never truly loved Him.

They were willing for a time to associate with Jesus in order to get what they wanted or needed, but that was all.

Jesus knew that they would behave that way. But it still had to have hurt!

"But Jesus on his part did not entrust himself to them, because he knew all people and needed no one to bear witness about man, for he himself knew what was in man." John 2:24-25

He knew what was IN MAN!

Isn't that at least part of our problem? We shouldn't be negative towards people, and Jesus never was—but He trusted God, not men.

He knew His disciples would flee like scared rabbits when the soldiers came and arrested Him so He didn't sit around crying about it. But it still had to have hurt!

As He looked out on the crowd mocking Him at least He saw John staring back.

At least His mother was still there.

But mostly all that He saw were angry, ungrateful, people who did not care how much He loved them.

He was truly tempted, and suffered in every imaginable way so that He could have compassion on you in what you have suffered.

His suffering did not stop Him from being compassionate; if anything it increased His compassion!

He was full of mercy and compassion in His ministry to people. On one occasion Jesus and the disciples were trying to get away from the crowds. Getting into the ships they made for the far side of the lake, but when they reached the other side the people were standing there by the thousands waiting on Him.

Instead of getting back in the ships and trying it again the bible tells us that; *"When he went ashore he saw a great crowd, and he had compassion on them and healed their sick."* Matthew 14:14.

Compassion alludes to kindness and sympathy, but there is something deeper, something even more profoundly powerful, in its meaning.

The origin of the word helps us grasp the true breadth and significance of compassion. In Latin, *'compati'* means *"suffer with."*

Compassion means someone else's heartbreak becomes your heartbreak. Another's suffering becomes your suffering.

True compassion changes the way we live.

You cannot have compassion on others and DO NOTHING!

God looked at this sin-sick world and was MOVED WITH COMPASSION!

That compassion caused God to send His only begotten Son to suffer and die in our place.

Jesus came to suffer and to die! That was His mission.

He came to show the world the love of God and to die for the lost.

Only great love could have caused Jesus to put up with the abuse.

Many people lose their compassion for others because of their sufferings, BUT NOT JESUS!

His compassion only grew stronger as He suffered. His sufferings were not His primary focus! Helping others and pleasing His Father were what defined Him in life and in death.

That is why He was anxious to save the thief at His side!

Instead of being bitter Jesus let His mercy flow out just as He allowed His blood to be shed.

He did this so that you and I could find in Him a Savior who understands and cares.

*"**We do not have a high priest who is unable to sympathize with our weaknesses**, but one who in every respect has been tempted as we are, yet without sin. Let us then with confidence draw near to the throne of grace, that we may receive mercy and find grace to help in time of need."* Hebrews 4:15-16

No matter what you have suffered it doesn't compare with the suffering of the Lord Jesus.

But don't let that make you think that He doesn't care deeply for your suffering—**this isn't a competition to see who suffered the most!**

Instead you should understand that He suffered so much in order to fully understand what we feel, what we suffer, and the depths of our despair.

He was tempted in all points, yet without sin!

He understands you and He knows all about you—yet He loves you anyway!

As the apostle Paul put it so beautifully, He became us!

*"**For such an high priest became us,** who is holy, harmless, undefiled, separate from sinners, and made higher than the heavens!"* Hebrews 7:26

He became us!!! Never forget that powerful truth!

Chapter 2: When people get hurt.

> *"You can accept or reject the way you are treated by other people, but until you heal the wounds of your past, you will continue to bleed. You can bandage the bleeding with food, with alcohol, with drugs, with work, with cigarettes, with sex, but eventually, it will all ooze through and stain your life."* — **Iyanla Vanzant, Yesterday I Cried.**

Let's understand this clearly—all wounds are meant to be healed! God sent Jesus to suffer and endure what He did so that we might find in Him our healing.

But it sometimes seems as if some wounds never heal.

Can Jesus truly heal ALL WOUNDS? The answer is yes, He heals all. But we have to actually surrender it to Him. Unless we give Jesus our hurts and pains He can't reach them to heal them.

He stands at the door of our hearts and knocks, but only we can open the door and let Jesus in.

Almost all people suffer in some way. It is my opinion that everyone has their own particular battle to fight. Yours might be completely different than mine, but it is a fight nonetheless.

In this chapter I want to deal with hurts; physical and emotional.

We all have our battles, but what we do when fighting that battle will make all of the difference in our lives.

When we suffer physically;

Suffering for many people is a normal part of life, no matter how much we might resist that fact. Some of the greatest soldiers of the cross have suffered greatly. Their commitment to Christ has not shielded them from hardships.

If you are one of those soldiers I want you to know that you are not alone, nor or you the only one who fights that kind of battle.

If you are in great pain from a sickness you should take courage, because the Great Physician is still the healer.

Also if you are incapacitated by an affliction you can be sure that Jesus will be there with you.

Remember the encouraging word that God spoke to the Apostle Paul in 2Corinthians 12:9 *"My grace is sufficient for you, for my power is made perfect in weakness."*

Paul took heart and said, *"Therefore I will boast all the more gladly of my weaknesses, so that the power of Christ may rest upon me. For the sake of Christ, then, I am content with weaknesses, insults, hardships, persecutions, and calamities. For when I am weak, then I am strong."* 2 Corinthians 12:9-10.

Here is the reason why I bring this up—it is our ability to surrender to Christ' power that is important. In our weakness He is made strong in us.

We find more grace in surrender than we do in resisting.

You are in great company, for many other saints have walked the same road that you walk.

Joni Eareckson Tada speaks of the great suffering that she has endured in her life

"In Deuteronomy 31:6, God tells me, "Be strong and courageous. Do not be afraid or terrified [of quadriplegia, chronic pain, or cancer], for the Lord your God goes with you; he will never leave you nor forsake you" (NIV).

"I'm convinced **a believer can endure any amount of suffering as long as he's convinced that God is with him in it. And we have the Man of Sorrows, the most God-forsaken man who ever lived**, so that, in turn, He might say to us, "I will never leave you; I will never forsake you."

"God wrote the book on suffering and He called it Jesus. This means God understands. He knows. He's with me."

She writes with depth about suffering because she has gone deep with Christ in suffering.

Over 100 years ago **Horatius Bonar**, the Scottish pastor wrote a little book called **Night of Weeping, or, When God's Children Suffer.**

In it he said his goal was, "to minister to the saints . . . to seek to bear their burdens, to bind up their wounds, and to dry up at least some of their many tears."

It is a great book to read for any who are suffering. He gives great Christian insights into how to process and profit by the things that we suffer.

In it he says, *"It is written by one who is seeking himself to profit by trial, and trembles lest it should pass by as the wind over the rock, leaving it as hard as ever; by one who would in every sorrow draw near to God that he may know Him more, and who is not unwilling to confess that as yet he knows but little."*

But this type of suffering is not uncommon to human beings. Our mortal bodies wear out in time and they ache and hurt. Sometimes tragedy strikes and leaves someone in terrible pain. It isn't God's will, but it happens.

There are also times when we as believers suffer for the cause of Christ. We should expect that to happen.

The promise of the Bible is that God's people will suffer persecution.

For example;

"Through many tribulations we must enter the kingdom." Acts 14:22

And Jesus said, *"If they persecuted me, they will persecute you"* John 15:20.

And Peter said, *"Do not be surprised at the fiery ordeal among you, which comes upon you for your testing, as though some strange thing were happening to you"* 1 Peter 4:12.

In other words it is not strange; it is to be expected.

And Paul said in 2 Timothy 3:12, *"Indeed, all who desire to live godly in Christ Jesus will be persecuted."*

It should not surprise us when the world hates us. We actually should expect the world to hate us! Jesus told us it would.

But there is another type of suffering that is not to be expected; and that is <u>when the attacks come from within</u>—from family, church and friends. Those attacks wound us far deeper than if it were done by enemies.

We have a right to think that the church will love its own kind! When another believer or friend or family hurts us it is different than any other hurt

When those we love and trust betray that trust it wounds us so deeply that it is hard to get over. A fellow believer doing us wrong has the tendency to drive us away from the Lord. We wrongly associate Him with those who claim to belong to Him and that is not fair. He did not harm us—that person did.

You must not think that what they did was from God for He never condoned or wanted them to do anything of the sort. We must separate the evil men from the God they misrepresent. You can't blame God; He is innocent.

We should expect to suffer in this world, but such suffering is from outsiders—unbelievers. It shouldn't come from fellow church members.

When that happens to us the first time it can shake our faith in God. It hurts deeply and we can't understand it.

I suspect that all of us have been in that place where our hearts cried out to our heavenly Father and asked that one word question of *"**Why?**"*

We are like a little child with tears in its eyes looking up at Daddy and weeping, **"Why?"**

When we ask God "**Why**" it is not just a question concerning right and wrong, it is a question of loyalty and relationship with God. We are crying out for affirmation that He is still our Father and we are still His children. Unless we are certain of our relationship with God we will never be able to come to grips with our present situation.

You can have a strong relationship with God and the whole world is against you! Everything hinges on that relationship!

So when we ask, *"But Father, why did this have to happen?"* we are not disparaging Him, we are speaking from the place of His child asking a legitimate question.

It is a legitimate question, and one that <u>God will answer</u>. But God answers <u>according to our ability to hear</u>, not according to our demand that He answer. <u>If we can't comprehend the answer He will not give it</u>.

What we need is not so much explanations as reassurances. And that is what we get: the reassurance of the Father in the person of Jesus, *"he who has seen me has seen the Father"* <u>John 14:9</u>.

I am sure that Martha and Mary wanted to know why Jesus didn't hurry to be with Lazarus when he needed Him the most. Jesus never answered the cries of their hearts.

Instead He raised Lazarus from the dead. However they still had to suffer and weep and wonder for over 4 days!

All of their questions evaporated as soon as Jesus spoke life back into their brother.

Beloved, our answer is not just a word **but the Word;** not an idea but a person.

He came!

He entered space and time and suffering.

The Song of Solomon describes Him as a lover. Love seeks above all intimacy, presence, togetherness.

As the old song says, *"I'd rather live in his world than to live without him in mine!"* That describes the way Jesus viewed us—He would rather suffer and die in our world than to enjoy an eternity in Heaven without us.

He came!

That is the main fact, the towering truth that keeps us from quitting when the world shouts at us to just give up.

He came!

He came to Job. And Job was satisfied even though the God who came gave him absolutely no answers at all to his thousand tortured questions. He did the most important thing and he gave the most important gift: himself. It is a lover's gift.

Out of our tears, our waiting, our darkness, our agonized aloneness, out of our weeping and wondering, out of our cry, "My God, my God, why hast Thou forsaken me?" **he came,** all the way, right to that cry.

So whatever wounds and hurts you have you must take them to Jesus. Only He will understand.

But the worst wounds are those we receive from our friends and family. That makes us suffer in ways that God never intended for us to suffer.

Jesus understands those hurts better than anyone.

We don't want to think that our friends will turn against us.

We don't want to believe that a family member will do us harm.

We refuse to accept that our church family doesn't always love us.

But sometimes we are wrong. **Sometimes we do get wounded in the house of our friends.**

Jesus knows all about that beloved. He can give you comfort in that lonely place because He walked through it first.

He sits beside us in the lowest places of our lives. Are we broken? He is broken with us. Are we rejected? Do people despise us not for our evil but for our good, or attempted good? He was *"despised and rejected of men."*

He was *"a man of sorrows and acquainted with grief."* Do people misunderstand us, turn away from us? They hid their faces from him as from an outcast, a leper.

Is our love betrayed? Are our tenderest relationships broken? He too loved and was betrayed by the ones he loved. *"He came unto his own and his own received him not."*

Does it ever feel as if life has passed us by or cast us out? Does it ever feel as if we are sinking into uselessness and oblivion? He sinks with us.

He comes down into that pit and gets a hold of our hands and pulls us out.

A pastor friend of mine was working on a septic tank when he dropped one of his tools into it. As badly as he needed that tool there was no way that he was going to reach down into that *"stuff"* and feel around for it! He remarked that he didn't love his tool that much.

But beloved, the King of the Universe did reach down into the muck and mire of your world to find you! He didn't just reach down—He came down! He came right to where we live in the darkest of the dark places!

He reached through our sin and through our misery to grab us and to pull us out.

We are that precious to Him!

He knows what it is to be passed over by the world. He knows rejection. He didn't run from it—He embraced it. And He told us to embrace it too.

But His way of suffering love is rejected by even some of his own followers.

It is abundantly clear that Jesus expects His followers to have the same care for one another that He had for us. **We are to love His people.**

When Jesus spoke these words to His disciples they were also intended for us; *"Anyone who has seen me has seen the Father!"* John 14:9.

What did the Lord mean by that statement? I believe that He intended for us to take it very literally!

When Jesus wept over Jerusalem He wasn't experiencing something foreign to the Father!

When Jesus' heart broke at Lazarus' tomb He wasn't doing something that God couldn't feel and comprehend.

When the Lord cried out with strong crying and tears in the Garden of Gethsemane the Father felt everything the Son felt!

He was no stranger to our tears and neither is the Father.

When you see Jesus you see the tears that flow from the heart of the Father.

And when one of His children are wounded, hurt or harmed He feels it personally.

God created the church, so that hurting people could have a place to find healing. Where two or three are gathered together in the name of Jesus He is right there in the middle of them.

Church is supposed to be the place where the love of God can be poured out like oil on the wounded hearts and lives of God's people.

It is the place where those who love us gather.

If there is any place that we should expect good instead of evil it would be in the presence of those who profess to love us. Yet often times it is the very ones we know and love which hurt us the worst and can stab us the deepest.

Perhaps there is no worse feeling in the world than to be betrayed by one's own family. From childhood on we learn to depend on and trust our parents and siblings. So when a family member betrays that trust it hurts us more than if a neighbor does it.

As we grow older we are all wounded by friends and school-mates. Some of the taunts and insults are hard to shake, and some children never seem to be able to get rid of them.

I have witnessed bold, outgoing children shrink back and become reclusive after being wounded by the words and actions of people they barely know.

Children are committing suicide because people they have never even met are ridiculing and insulting them online.

Let's face it, words hurt.

You may have followed a story in the news about how a teenage girl convinced her boyfriend to kill himself through a series of harsh and unrelenting text messages.

She bullied and persuaded him into acting on his suicidal thoughts. She even accused him of being weak when he had second thoughts and tried to back out of it.

He eventually went through with it and killed himself, but she was partly to blame. He would have stopped several times but she pushed him until he finally gave in.

The boy himself trusted his girlfriend's words: *"You'll be better off," "You must do it." "Don't be a coward!" "No more waiting."*

She pushed him until he followed through and committed suicide.

Words can hurt, and sometimes, words can kill.

Grown adults can still recall the exact words and phrases that demeaned and wounded them in childhood. And when they do, they are still overcome with the same feelings that they felt the day that it happened.

I have sat with octogenarians in nursing homes who were broken hearted over something that happened to them when they were children! It still hurts!

The words still hurt because they were spoken by people who supposedly loved them.

The offense is still fresh because it wounded their innocent souls.

You can wound a child for life!

All it takes is one act to ruin their psyche and change their personality for the rest of their lives.

Children are far more trusting than adults are and therefore can be hurt worse.

As we grow older we usually gain in our capacity to not let harmful sayings affect us. Gradually we pull in our emotions and keep a safe guard on our heart so that we can't be hurt as easily.

A cocoon may be a good thing for a caterpillar, but it is harmful for people. We may avoid being hurt, but we avoid being able to interact with others as well.

What is worse is that in our isolation we unintentionally force ourselves to relive our hurts because we lack newer inputs. The only thing we tend to know is the past with its hurts.

Facing and defeating our fears is a large part of growing up. Unless we can do that we will forever be stunted in our spiritual and emotional maturity.

As we grow and become involved in group activities we also open ourselves up to being wounded.

People who get hurt tend to go one of two ways; they either get calloused to being hurt or they constantly quit each time someone says something mean to them.

But what happens when the wounds are inflicted in church?

Church is supposed to be a safe place. It is where you should feel accepted and loved no matter who you are and what you have been doing.

Church is the body of Jesus Christ on earth. He lives and loves and moves through His body to reach, teach and heal His sheep.

We are able to grow closer to God in corporate worship than we are able to alone. That is on purpose! God wants the body to come together.

But not all Christians are completely healed.

In every church there are people who have never healed from past hurts. There are also people who are abusive. And then the devil puts some of his people in church too.

The reality is that you can be wounded in church just like the world.

If you could go through any town or city in America and gather people together who have been driven out of church by things Christians have done there wouldn't be enough buildings to house them all!

As with our immediate family we expect to be able to let down our guard and relax in peace with our church family. Sadly that is not always possible.

There are exceptions of course.

There are churches which simply permeate the love of God! Where you can come broken, bruised and smelling of a hog-pen and they will wrap their arms around you and bring you to the Father.

Thank God for those churches!

But the real danger that lurks is that all too many churches and more specifically the leadership simply refuses to correct or even to restrict vicious and mean people.

Many times leaders prefer to ignore harmful antics in the hopes that nobody will be wounded too badly.

We have probably all heard the excuses of *"Oh, that's just how old brother Snakeinthegrass is!"* or *"You can't take Sister Bitesalot too seriously!"*

What that tells you is that the leadership is afraid of those people. It is easier to allow them to cause a little trouble now than a lot of trouble later. But that is cowardice!

People are being driven out of some churches faster than the pastor can get new ones in! And in the vast majority of cases they aren't going out to a different church, they are simply quitting church altogether. The devil is having a heyday because leaders are afraid to lead!

<u>Many years ago</u> I was working in a place that had predominantly female workers. One young woman who worked there was extremely loud and fairly obnoxious. I was attempting to befriend her and trying to witness to her about Jesus.

As I talked to her one day about serving the Lord she abruptly shut me off and with fire in her eyes explained to me why she didn't want anything to do with church or God.

When she was about 12 she went to a small church. A deacon there began to take an interest in her. She was uncomfortable but nobody seemed to notice or care that he was always touching her, feeling her hair, hugging on her and being very "handsy" to her.

One day he pulled her into a room at church and molested her. Feeling shocked and scared out of her wits she left for home and never again could be talked into going to church.

You see, **for her church equaled shame**, hurt, regrets and indifference. When she thought of church she thought of the worst day of her life when the worst thing in her life happened.

The leadership of that church was indifferent to her suffering. Indifference on the part of those whom God had appointed to guard the most helpless members of the flock led directly to this young girl being wounded for life. **She never looked at church as the answer to her problems;** *it represented the cause of all of her griefs.*

My heart broke for her as she told me this story. Her hurt was still fresh and her shame was still there. Tears streamed down her face as she confided in me what had happened.

I felt a seething anger at the devilish man who was a deacon—a leader in the church! How could a man who was charged with helping to lead the sheep do such a thing?

With tears in my eyes I told her that God was hurt when she was hurt. He had placed people in her life to protect her and they had all failed in their duties to her and God.

Her parents, her relatives, the people in the church who ignored that old pervert and most importantly her pastor had all failed her.

For whatever reason they chose to turn a blind eye to that man's obvious perverted behavior. No man should be petting and caressing a little girl not his own. That constant touching is something that SOMEONE should have put a stop to.

It is very likely that because he was a deacon he had family behind him and that made him feel as if he was above others. His wicked heart was not worried about anyone confronting him.

I explained to the girl that I fully understood her feelings of shame and panic every time that she even thought about going to church. It represented everything bad that had happened to her.

But I assured her that Jesus wasn't the one who attacked her. It was the devil who had done that. So the fact that she refused to come to Jesus was actually her standing alongside of the one who had harmed her.

With a look of surprise she responded that she had never thought of it that way. She ended up giving her heart to the Lord and He began the healing process.

I wish I could say that she just put it all behind her and enjoyed her life, but that is not true.

Wounds sometimes last for years.

Some might be there until we die. She did recover some and heal some. She is closer to God than she was, but that attack has changed her fundamentally.

It is not as if she can just pretend it didn't happen.

Her emotional state is different because of what happened way back when she was a child.

Her personality was shaped by that incident.

The way that she interacts with her husband and children is different than it would have been if she had not had to endure so much grief and torment at the hands of that wicked man.

You see, **it is not possible to undo an offense.**

Once it is done it is done. Prayer accomplishes much and God can pick up the broken pieces and put you back together again, but those old hurts will always be there in measure.

He can strengthen you to where they do not dictate to you how to live, love or feel, but it will always be a scar that you will cause you to remember.

Words spoken harshly cannot be unspoken, a punch cannot be withdrawn.

Once we let ourselves say or do something that causes someone else harm it is done. It is far better to not do something than to do it and regret it forever.

That young woman surprised me one Sunday morning. I was so happy when she and her husband came to our church.

It was very difficult for her and you could see the nervousness in her eyes, but she pushed through her fears and came.

That day God showered her with His presence and she began to heal.

It was the first in a long series of steps, but God will get her there in time.

We all have opportunities to do someone good to someone or to harm them. Oftentimes we do one or the other by what we say. Our words can cut like a knife if we're not careful.

I have listened as people from other churches speak out loud about how withdrawn their pastor's wife has become. The insinuation is that she is haughty, or stuck-up.

Ignorantly they tried to fill in the gaps on why they thought she acted that way. Not one of them had a clue to the kinds of insults and ridicule that poor woman has had to endure as part of her ministry.

Many pastors' and their wives suffer in private. It is impossible to directly refute every insult, and in the end they know it is self-defeating to try.

A soldier may be triggered by the sound of fireworks. **Many pastors are triggered by the sound of a phone!**

Every ring sends chills down their spines; will it be more bad news, griping, fault finding and complaining? They tense up even before they answer the phone!

Trauma has a way of affecting everything that the wounded people do; how they think, react, and interact with others.

It becomes easy to withdraw and to hide their feelings. They insulate themselves to keep from being hurt.

I actually believe that many of them suffer from **PTSD— post traumatic stress disorder** or something very similar.

They might behave like people in shock when confronted with a reminder of their past hurt.

For them a sort of numbness has set in where they simply go through life without being able to enjoy it.

They are waiting for the next trigger that starts them hurting again and living in dread of it.

That young woman had lived with that one incident for over 20 years and yet it was still fresh to her. It still made her shake as she recounted to me the awfulness of what happened. Tears of hurt still flowed as she faced it once again.

She had not healed. She could not escape it. She needed help which only Jesus could bring, **and she associated Him with church** so to her mind He wasn't an option either.

According to the Mayo Clinic, PTSD is *"is a mental health condition that's triggered by a terrifying event — either experiencing it or witnessing it. Symptoms may include flashbacks, nightmares and severe anxiety, as well as uncontrollable thoughts about the event. Most people who go through traumatic events may have temporary difficulty adjusting and coping. If the symptoms get worse, last for months or even years, and interfere with your day-to-day functioning,* **you may have PTSD.**"

PTSD is the minds way of trying to survive something that it is not made to handle.

One young boy witnessed his dad beating his mother every day. He would scream at him to please stop and then he would turn on the boy and beat him senseless. Now when anyone raises their voices he winces. He can't help it.

That kind of traumatic experience sticks with us and shapes us.

The people who are suffering from past traumas can't just put it away—they need healing. And the only real Healer is Jesus Christ.

That is why the devil works so hard to keep church from operating as it should. The devil knows the power inherit in a Holy Spirit led church, He knows that it will bring healing and deliverance to those who are held in captivity. That is why he fights so hard to bring turmoil and confusion into the body.

We are in a fallen world filled with hurting and fallen people. We shouldn't expect it to be peaceful for everyone.

The devil doesn't play fair; he will hurt you, lie on you, cheat on you, slander you and he will get his people to do his dirty work.

If you are not ready for the constant barrage of attacks that the devil and his crowd can lob at you it can quickly overwhelm you.

Some people just have never had to deal with such things before and they can't cope.

And because so many who should protect them refuse to do so they are left confused and hurt.

Sadly there are millions of walking wounded among us who would love to have God wrap His big strong arms around them but they are so wounded they don't know how to get to Him or to yield to His Spirit.

Perhaps you are one of those wounded people?

Please consider what you are about to read carefully;

Do you have recurrent unwanted distressing memories?

Do you relive the traumatic event as if it were happening again (*flashbacks)?*

Do you ever have unsettling dreams or nightmares about the traumatic event?

Do you ever suffer from severe emotional distress or physical reactions to something that reminds you of the traumatic event?

If so you classify as suffering from PTSD.

If you do it is affecting every part of your life.

Your interaction with others is affected. There is no way it cannot be. You have a wound that you are going to protect any way that you know how.

That means that you are going to guard that wound against anyone touching it, seeing it or speaking of it. You guard it by how you react when confronted with it.

Unconsciously perhaps you might get angry or emotional any time something forces you to relive the agony of your experience.

You will find that your relationship even with God is affected.

Whether you blame Him or not you have a wound that is still there and you haven't received healing for it yet. How you interact with God, how you pray or worship, they are all connected.

If you have something in your heart that is not healed it is stopping God from completing His work in your life. He will deal with that wound if you won't. He is a healer and He will not just ignore a gaping wound in your psyche.

It often occurs that wounded people who refuse to deal with their hurts end up hurting themselves and those they love.

It is better to deal with the pain and be done with it than to carry it around for the rest of your life.

Being attacked can cause you to change your way of thinking. I have known outgoing and charismatic people to withdraw and become reclusive after being wounded by other people. Their thinking changed. Their outlook changed. They became different people than they used to be.

It is all too common.

If it were a cut or a broken bone you would go to a doctor or hospital and have it taken care of, but a wounded soul is not so easy to heal.

Only Jesus can heal the soul, and the devil will work overtime to keep you away from Him.

Do you routinely deal with the following things?

Negative thoughts about yourself, other people or the world

Hopelessness about the future

Memory problems, including not remembering important aspects of the traumatic event

Difficulty maintaining close relationships

Feeling detached from family and friends

Lack of interest in activities you once enjoyed

Difficulty experiencing positive emotions

Feeling emotionally numb

If that describes you then you are in need of healing so that you can get your life back. Until you have healing in this area you will be stuck where you are.

I mentioned PTSD earlier. **It is important that we understand that it is a normal reaction to trauma.**

It doesn't mean that you are weak or mentally unstable because you have a difficult time coming to grips with trauma.

Some of the signs of trauma induced stress are;

Being easily startled or frightened or always being on guard for danger. Self-destructive behavior. Trouble sleeping. Trouble concentrating. Irritability, angry outbursts or aggressive behavior. Overwhelming guilt or shame

All of these behaviors are self-destructive which only goes to prove that the devil is behind them.

The devil came to steal, kill and to destroy. John 10:10.

Jesus came that we might have life, and have it more abundantly!

In this book I want to shed light on abuse in the church and among Christians towards other Christians. The reason for this is;

1. ***To help the wounded find healing in Jesus***

2. ***And to force pastors and leaders to put a stop to bullies and abusive people destroying innocent lives in their congregations.***

There is hope for those who have been hurt and wounded!

Jesus is still the healer and the Redeemer. He can and He will help.

Solomon said, *"To all the living there is hope!"* Ecclesiastes 9:4.

No matter how much you may have suffered or how far in the pit you may have sunk—there is still hope for you in Christ!

If you have been hurt deeply by your family, church or friends take heart—Jesus identifies with you. You and others like you belong to a group of which He is the Leader. He knows everything that you feel, think and wish.

Do not despair for <u>the Champion</u> is on your side.

Chapter 3: Skandal

Before we get started, let me assure you that I know the word "*scandal*" is spelled with a *"C."*

However in the Greek it is spelled with a *"K."* The reason why I used the Greek spelling is actually very important.

Skandal is found throughout the New Testament.

The Lord Jesus spoke much about it, for instance here;

*"Whoever shall receive one such little child in My name receives Me. But whoever **shall offend** (Skandal) one of these little ones who believes in Me, it would be better for him that a millstone were hung around his neck, and he be sunk in the depth of the sea."* Matthew 18:5-6

Lest anyone try to soften the Lord's warning let me assure you that He meant every word that He spoke!

Can you imagine the horror of being tied to a heavy stone and then being dropped into the deepest sea?

Well that would be better than facing the Lord Jesus after bringing harm to His bride the church!

He said that anyone who **Skandalized** *"One of these little ones"* would suffer for it. He made no exceptions! He accepts no excuses either!

To really understand the meaning of this verse we need to understand what skandal means.

"Skandal" according to Dr. Thayer's Definition:

1) To put a stumbling block or impediment in the way, upon which another may trip and fall, metaphorically to offend

1a) to entice to sin

1b) to cause a person to begin to distrust and desert one whom he ought to trust and obey

1b1) to cause to fall away

When that young girl was molested at 12 years of age she was "***Skandalized***."

That man *"put a stumbling block in her way to keep her from getting to Jesus. He caused her to fall away from the Lord. He made her more comfortable in sin than in God's presence. She no longer trusted in Christ."*

So on the Day of Judgement that man will answer for more than just that one solitary act; he will answer for all of the harm that his action caused.

And keep in mind that the whole chain of events started in his wicked heart and the people who should have been protecting that little girl didn't want to get involved.

Sin—lust—starts in the heart.

"But each person is tempted when he is lured and enticed by his own desire. Then desire when it has conceived gives birth to sin, and sin when it is fully grown brings forth death." James 1:14-15

It is the hidden sins that people refuse to acknowledge or to deal with that are the root cause of all wrongful acts. And that hidden sin exists because they fail to take them to the altar and come clean with God.

We all have a sinful nature, and it is only by leaning on the Lord Jesus and letting the Holy Spirit control us that we can overcome it. **BUT WE CAN OVERCOME IT!**

If lusts persist in us it is because we feed them and allow them to stay.

The deacon who molested that young girl didn't just happen to do that out of the blue. It was in his wicked heart for a long time before he actually went through with it.

How can a man who willfully harms or destroys a young girl just to satisfy his perverted desires justify that act to Jesus Christ?

I have spoken with people on both sides; a man who committed those types of atrocities and just wanted to be forgiven and have it forgotten, and the victim who can never get closure because her innocence was taken away.

How exactly do we reconcile such behavior?

The only way is to be 100% honest, and quite frankly, most people lack the courage to be that brutally honest.

It is too easy for the perpetrator to say, *"Well, they instigated it! They deserved what they got!"*

Nobody ever deserved to be raped or attacked.

Someone was supposed to be the protecting adult.

There is zero chance that Jesus will look that person in the eye and say, *"Well, you have a point."*

No sir! He will say, *"You knew better! To him who knows to do good and does it not to him it is sin!"* James 4:17

He will lay it squarely at their feet and make them explain it and take ownership of it.

Each of us will answer for what WE HAVE DONE!

You cannot make me sin! No one can make us sin!

If I sin it is solely because I had the sin in my heart to begin with.

"What comes out of the mouth proceeds from the heart, and this defiles a person. For out of the heart come evil thoughts, murder, adultery, sexual immorality, theft, false witness, slander. These are what defile a person." Matthew 15:18-20

In this day we live the internet is available to almost everyone and it is the cesspool in which many men and women have fallen. On it there is a ready supply of every sick and vile thing to feed the lusts and evil in their hearts.

It is only a matter of time until the thoughts become actions.

What you think of most is what you will eventually allow yourself to do.

This is true of acts of violence, lust and revenge. If you dwell on it long enough you will eventually act on it.

The Lord said that thinking it in our hearts is equal to doing the very act.

"But I say to you that everyone who looks at a woman with lustful intent has already committed adultery with her in his heart." Matthew 5:28

The point is if we allow sin to gain a stronghold in our hearts we will eventually act on it. The lustful desires will eventually manifest into actions.

If you harbor hatred in your heart towards anyone you block the Holy Spirit from changing you and making you a strong Christian. That hatred takes root and grows! It never stays small! It eventually will get too big for you to control.

Sin in the heart will take you places you never dreamed you would go and will make you do horrible things that you never imagined that you would be capable of doing.

"Lust when it has conceived gives birth to sin, and sin when it is fully grown brings forth death." **James 1:15.**

It may stay hidden for a long time, but eventually lust in the heart will manifest into death in your life.

By death I mean that it will kill relationships with people and with God.

It will kill your future that God wants you to have.

It will kill your dreams and ambitions

As one man said, *"Sin will take you further than you wanted to go. Slowly but wholly taking control. Sin will leave you longer than you want to stay. Sin will cost you far more than you want to pay."*

Hidden sins manifest eventually.

The following true story illustrates this truth. Even though they were thought of as leaders, the two men I mention were hypocrites who destroyed a weaker brother.

Many years ago I had a friend who I was able to help lead to the Lord.

He began to attend a local church and was doing well.

He had never been to church so he wasn't versed on what was and was not permissible. He didn't dress up to code and his language was still rough. But he was sincerely trying to live a life pleasing to the Lord.

One day he was putting shingles on his roof when he accidently hit his thumb with the hammer. It hurt something awful and he instantly let out a curse word.

He no sooner said it than he apologized to God and asked Him to help him never say that again.

Actually for a new believer that is commendable.

However on Sunday he went to Sunday school and asked the teacher if he was alright with God or if he had backslidden.

A mature Christian would have understood his dilemma and would have encouraged him to keep on going and not let it grieve him. He repented immediately. He had done the right thing.

But not every person in church is mature.

The teacher of the class and another man both condemned him for uttering one solitary curse word.

They said to him *"if you were truly saved that would never have come out of your mouth in the first place!"*

My friend was devastated! He thought he was saved, but now he learned that he had never been—***at least according to those two men.*** He left the church and never went back.

I found out what happened and went to see him. I found him in a bar, drinking a beer. With tears in his eyes he told me that he was never saved because he let out a curse word. I assured him that he had been saved and that God still loved him. With everything I knew I tried to convince him to return to the Lord. I assured him that God would restore him, but it was no use. They had destroyed the weak brother.

The bible tells us that the strong should take care of the weak;

"We who are strong have an obligation to bear with the failings of the weak." Romans 15:1

It would have been easy for those two men to have encouraged him, but they never even considered it! They were self-righteous frauds who enjoyed feeling superior to a weaker person.

I knew both men very well. I was so disappointed to find that they had spoken anything into his life.

One was an avowed racist who regularly spewed hatred out of his mouth. His heart was wicked and it showed.

The other secretly was an alcoholic. He drank whiskey which he hid under his car seat. He also had molested one of his daughters.

They were not in any position to pass judgment on anyone! But they did.

Those two hypocrites were allowed to pass judgment on a sincere believer.

Out of the abundance of the heart the mouth speaks!

Poisonous attitudes spring from poisonous hearts.

You might say, *"Well pastor won't that man have to answer to the Lord for leaving the church?"*

Yes, of course he will. And for all eternity he will remember that I went into a bar to get him.

BUT HE WOULD NEVER HAVE BEEN THERE IN THE FIRST PLACE WITHOUT THOSE TWO MEN!

It is doubtful that either of those two hypocrites even thought about the fact that they destroyed that man. I doubt if they have ever lost any sleep thinking about his eternal destiny that they helped alter.

But the Lord saw it all! And He keeps accurate records.

It is a principle—a law if you will—that no sin stays private. Sooner or later it will affect others in your life.

A man told me that he didn't feel the least bit convicted by drinking a beer now and then.

I asked him to consider the following scenario;

"Let's suppose that you go into a Wal-Mart to buy your beer. There you run into a new member of the church who just happens to be a recovering alcoholic.

For years he put his family through a living hell!

There is no way to describe the suffering that they were forced to endure because of his drinking.

But then he came to church and got saved! God instantly delivered him from the desire to drink and now his family is happy and whole.

But he sees you with a six-pack of beer!

He is a weaker brother, new in the Lord. He is going to think that if you can drink now and then and you think it is ok then surely he can too.

And soon he is drinking again—this brother for whom Christ died is again going down that road to destruction.

Soon enough he isn't just drinking a beer now and then, he is back to getting so drunk that he again is mean to his family and friends.

His family is the first to suffer, and when they plead with him to stop he mentions YOUR NAME! He tells them that YOU DRINK and its ok.

YOU have sent him and his family back to a living hell.

His wife finally has enough and seeing no other remedy because church has failed her, she leaves him and takes the children.

<u>All of that happened because YOU DRANK!</u>

Was it really worth it?"

The man looked at me stunned for a minute.

Then his eyes showed anger!

He told me that he wasn't responsible for what other people did!

He said that he was only responsible for himself.

But is that true?

According to the bible we are very responsible for the souls of others!

"In humility count others more significant than yourselves. Let each of you look not only to his own interests, but also to the interests of others." Philippians 2:3-4

"Love is patient and kind. It does not insist on its own way." 1Corinthians 13:4-5

"Let no one seek his own good, but the good of his neighbor." 1Corinthians 10:24

If what we do has a detrimental impact on others we will answer for it and we will answer to Jesus Himself!

In the first century there were many idols and temples associated with idols.

Most of the meat that was served in the markets had been sacrificed to idols.

When the Gentiles came out of idolatry and became Christians they stopped having anything to do with idols and that meant eating meat that had been offered to the idols.

The mature believers realized that the meat was not cursed. They could eat it without sinning.

But the immature believers couldn't separate the meat offered to an idol from the actual idol worship. To them it was one and the same.

So what was the Apostle Paul's advice?

*"For if anyone sees you who have knowledge eating in an idol's temple, will he not be encouraged, if his conscience is weak, to eat food offered to idols? And so by your knowledge this weak person is destroyed, the brother for whom Christ died. Thus, **sinning against your brothers** and wounding their conscience when it is weak, **you sin against Christ.**"* 1 Corinthians 8:10-12

If you sin against Jesus Christ who is there to plead your case to God the Father? Jesus is the only Mediator between God and man! You have alienated the only Lawyer allowed in God's presence!

By sinning against the weak we are cutting our own throats!

"You who are mature should not eat it because it would possibly destroy a weak brother!"

That is all you need to know!

If it would hurt someone then I shouldn't do it!!!!

As far as drinking goes, it is never good to put the devil into your mouth!

YOUR WITNESS AND YOUR TESTIMONY IS DESTROYED WHEN YOU PARTAKE OF ALCOHOL.

And it can potentially ruin someone else's life!

Why would we as true Christians even consider doing something that could potentially send another soul to hell? What kind of a Christian would even countenance such a thing?

The Apostle Paul said *"It is good not to eat meat or drink wine or do anything that causes your brother to stumble."* Romans 14:21

Do you as a Christian truly want to please the Lord?

Then stop trying to please yourself and become a servant to others!

Put others first!

Think of their needs first!

There is no reason for a believer to partake of any behavior that could cause anyone to lose out with God.

I mentioned that I once went into a bar to witness to my friend. I prayed and felt the Lord compel me to go, but of course I did not sit down, or drink and when it became apparent that I was not succeeding I left.

That was the only time I have ever set foot in a bar since I was saved in 1979.

Otherwise I will not go near such a place. It is the den of devils.

You might think that I am being judgmental. Well I was raised in bars. I have spent many days and nights in them. I know what they are and I recognize the atmosphere. It is devilish. No Christian should ever feel comfortable in the devil's home. The bible clearly tells us to be separate from the world;

"Do not be unequally yoked with unbelievers. For what partnership has righteousness with lawlessness? Or what fellowship has light with darkness? What accord has Christ with Belial? Or what portion does a believer share with an unbeliever? What agreement has the temple of God with idols?

For we are the temple of the living God; as God said, "I will make my dwelling among them and walk among them, and I will be their God, and they shall be my people. Therefore go out from their midst, and be separate from them, says the Lord, and touch no unclean thing; then I will welcome you, and I will be a father to you, and you shall be sons and daughters to me, says the Lord Almighty." 2 Corinthians 6:14-18

Do not be like the world! Do not try to please them, live like them, talk like them or be loved by them! Our goal should be to be always pleasing to the Lord.

If we can help someone we are commanded to. But that does not mean that we are to become sinners to win sinners.

We are the Temple of the Living God! That Temple is holy so we had better keep it holy in all of our conversations and actions.

We should always be seeking for a way to show the world our Savior. He should be visible in everything that we do or say. His love for us should compel us to love others also.

As the Apostle John said, *"If anyone has the world's goods and sees his brother in need, yet closes his heart against him, how does God's love abide in him?"* **1 John 3:17.**

That isn't just talking about giving food or water to someone in need. It is also talking about giving help or comfort to them.

If you harm them how can you honestly claim to have the love of God in your heart?

If you are hooked on pornography it will eventually manifest itself in your life. That lust will grow until it becomes an outward act.

A certain pastor and his staff somehow got the notion that they were so *"Mature"* that they could watch X-rated movies and it wouldn't harm them.

The results were predictable; every couple committed adultery and every couple divorced.

Their families were destroyed.

The church where they went was destroyed.

Other families in the church were destroyed.

Their children were and are messed up and confused.

And God's name was blasphemed.

You cannot partake of an obvious work of the flesh and it not have a negative impact on your life.

IF they had loved others and thought of them as *"better than themselves"* they would never have gone down that road of destruction. But they thought too highly of themselves and too little of others.

One member of that church asked me what had happened. He couldn't understand what went wrong. I explained to him what I knew first-hand.

With surprise in his eyes he said, *"I would never have believed that the pastor and his wife could have been so dumb!"*

Indeed, they should have known better than any that **you always reap exactly what you sow!**

Our life has to be an example for others to follow. If we please ourselves it shows that the love of God is not in us.

"Be humble and consider others more important than yourselves." Philippians 2:3

The Lord Jesus came to serve, not be served! Are we better than Him?

How do we condone trampling on weaker believers?

If we love God we MUST LOVE our brothers and sisters so intently that we will never even consider hurting them in any way.

"Let us not love in word or talk but in deed and in truth." 1John 3:18

Let us put our love into action!

"Love one another with brotherly affection. Outdo one another in showing honor." Romans 12:10

No normal person is going to try to do harm to his own brother. He will take up for him and protect him.

That is how we are supposed to see other believers.

We are to do everything in our power to keep the unity of the body. No believer is above others. We are all part of the same body.

I remember listening to worship in a college in Bangalore India. There were several different nationalities represented there and each group performed a worship song in their own dialect. It was wonderful! I never understood one solitary word but I recognized the Spirit!

They were my brothers and sisters just as much as if I had known them all of my life!

How could I do anything that would harm them?

It would be un-Christian of me to harm another Christian.

"Love works no ill to his neighbor: therefore love is the fulfilling of the law." Romans 13:10.

If you want to please God then you MUST LOVE GOD'S KIDS!!!!

If you don't love God's people how can you love God?

If you can't love them enough to put them ahead of yourself then what kind of a servant are you?

"If anyone says, "I love God," and hates his brother, he is a liar; *for he who does not love his brother whom he has seen cannot love God whom he has not seen."* <u>1John 4:20</u>

John separates the sheep from the goats pretty easily! If you love your brother you are of God. If you hate your brother you don't know God. Case closed!

Our supreme example is the Lord Jesus. He came to earth and became a servant, though He was God. He humbled Himself and served others when He was the rightful King and Ruler of planet earth and the heavens.

He could have demanded that people be subservient to Him, but He didn't. Instead Jesus served others.

"For I have given you an example that you also should do just as I have done to you." <u>John 13:15</u>

If He is our example then we cannot claim to be a follower of Jesus unless we walk in His footsteps. We must do what He did and serve others like He did.

"You know that the rulers of the Gentiles lord it over them, and their great ones exercise authority over them. It shall not be so among you. But whoever would be great among you must be your servant, and whoever would be first among you must be your slave, even as the Son of Man came not to be served but to serve, and to give his life as a ransom for many." <u>Matthew 20:25-28</u>

We are not to be like heathens! We should not seek to have others meet our needs, but we should be trying to strengthen the weak and hold up the feeble.

If we look at weaker people as annoyances that is not being Christ-like.

"I urge you to walk in a manner worthy of the calling to which you have been called, with all humility and gentleness, with patience, bearing with one another in love, eager to maintain the unity of the Spirit in the bond of peace." Ephesians 4:1-3

We should want to stand before the Lord with clean hands and a clean heart. If you can't do good then at least don't do harm!

If you have been saved then you know that the love of God was poured out on you and that God took you into His family.

If God showed you so much love shouldn't you show it to others? The bible says that we should.

"Beloved, if God so loved us, we also ought to love one another." 1 John 4:11

We should always be ready to show love and mercy to others, because we ourselves need love and mercy.

Try to out-love others!

"Let us consider how to stir up one another to love and good works." Hebrews 10:24

You can stir up others by setting a good example for them. It may not be popular and it will not make you famous on earth, but serving others is what Jesus would do if He were in your shoes.

Those are the people who walk with heaven's anointing.

I would rather have God's approval than to own a thousand mansions and a fleet of jets.

"For Christ did not please Himself!" Romans 15:3

Who should we love?

That's easy! Anyone that Jesus loved we should love!

Set an example for others to follow!

That way you can say what the Apostle Paul said;

"Brothers, join in imitating me, and keep your eyes on those who walk according to the example you have in us." Philippians 3:17

At the end of our lives we might be able to point out smarter people than us, richer people than us, more successful people than us, but we should never be able to find more loving people than we are.

If we are disciples of Christ then we should act like Him.

"A disciple is not above his teacher, nor a servant above his master. It is enough for the disciple to be like his teacher, and the servant like his master." Matthew 10:24-25

I have conducted more funerals than I can recall. Some were glorious as the presence of God would fill the hall where the service was conducted. I remember something about each of those services—none of the people who had died were famous! Not one! But each of them left an indelible mark on their world as a true believer in Jesus Christ.

When we die that is really all that will matter—did we know the Lord and did our lives match our words?

The first funeral I ever did was for a man who died at home. His family asked me if I believed that he had gone to heaven. I wish they had not asked, for I had to be honest. *"I wouldn't take his chances if it were me"* I said.

The greatest gift a father can give to his family after he's gone is for them to know beyond a doubt that he went to heaven.

Another funeral that I did was for a man who was bragged on by everyone there. He was a great man and as far as I could tell had no blemish to his name.

Yet years later I found out from his children that he had been a different man at home.

He routinely abused his children, even sexually, and then played the part of a Christian to the world.

Needless to say those children have a hard time getting close to God now.

To summarize this chapter let me just say this;

Do not harm anyone.

Put others first.

Be a servant to all and you will please God.

Live your life in a way that no pastor will be ashamed to preach your funeral.

Chapter 4: When church leaders fail

But Jesus said to him, "Judas, are you betraying the Son of Man with a kiss?" Luke 22:48

Jesus knew who would betray Him, but it still hurt. We often think of Jesus in superhuman terms, but He walked this earth **AS A MAN**. He laid aside His divinity when He came to earth to be born as a helpless baby.

What you feel **He felt!** When Judas betrayed Him into the hands of His enemies it hurt. It hurt because He knew what was about to become of Judas. He knew all about the path that Judas was on. Jesus knew Judas' end would be awful. Jesus loved Judas, so it hurt when His friend betrayed Him.

It hurt because He knew what was in store for Himself. He knew about the rejection, abuse and crucifixion that awaited Him.

Have you ever been betrayed by a close friend?

Do you remember the mental anguish that you felt?

Can you still feel the hurt at discovering that someone you loved, invested in, cared for and respected turned against you? Well Jesus felt all of that and more.

He felt the anguish of betrayal. Judas had been a close friend for over 3 years! Jesus had invested in Judas.

He had shown Judas that He trusted him by letting him be the treasurer. He loved Judas. He cared for Judas. He was deeply hurt for and by Judas.

Jesus knew personally what it is like to be betrayed, and He can help you when you feel that same hurt.

Jesus established the church. It is His body on earth. As such it is to be a hospital **FOR** the sick and wounded.

It was never intended to be the place where people **were made sick and wounded!**

The Lord created the church—it is His. And He has put people in place whose job it is to guard and protect the flock. If they do their jobs they will routinely make someone mad. Some might even leave the church and say terrible things about the leaders. This prospect freezes some God-appointed leaders and they refuse to do their duties.

One thing that every church **MUST HAVE** is strong leadership that is not afraid of man but is fearful of displeasing the Lord.

If we have people who are scared to death of offending a person but not the least bit worried about what God thinks we have chaos.

When that happens all hell is loosed upon a congregation!

When a pastor is paralyzed by the fear of losing his job or running off a good tithe payer he has lost his leadership and someone else is running the church.

When deacons are afraid of somebody of influence in the church and can't make any decision unless that influencer first approves of it they no longer run the church.

When that happens people are going to be hurt, and hurt bad.

Skandal

To a Greek speaking audience the word **skandal** meant something very specific.

Picture a mouse trap; if I was to set a trap and I caught a mouse in it, it would injure the mouse. Even if the mouse got away it would never be the same. It would probably have a broken bone or two. It may not be able to gather enough food to survive.

If it was a mother mouse that was caught then its offspring would suffer because of what I had done to their mother. They might all starve to death because of me.

To the Greek audience I would have "**skandalized**" that mouse.

It goes far deeper than just a single act—it included the RESULTS of that act also!

The sad truth is many people have been skandalized in the house of God.

If I offended or skandalized a person then what I have done will have many ramifications in that person's life.

If he walks away from Jesus I will have to answer to the Lord for that!

If he becomes sad, depressed, indifferent or hostile because of what I have done I will have to give an answer to the Lord for it.

If that person's life doesn't matter anymore to me than that how exactly can I prove that I love God or even know Him?

Here is an example of what I am speaking of;

A pastor was flirting with a married woman. She responded by flirting back.

Her husband found out and became very jealous. Eventually the couple separated and divorced. The woman ended up without a husband or the pastor; he wasn't about to give up his church for her.

Is the pastor guilty of more than lusting after a woman?

According to the bible he is guilty of causing everything that his actions brought about. **AND HE WILL ANSWER TO JESUS FOR IT!**

Jesus loves His people enough to die for them.

His love is from everlasting to everlasting. Don't you think that He takes it personally when one of His children is harmed?

"The King will answer them, 'Truly, I say to you, as you did it to one of the least of these my brothers, you did it to me. Then he will say to those on his left, 'Depart from me, you cursed, into the eternal fire prepared for the devil and his angels." Matthew 25:40-41

We cannot ignore the consequences of our actions. By allowing people to be wounded and worse in our midst we are sinning against Christ!

By *"Sinning against your brothers and wounding their conscience when it is weak, you sin against Christ."* 1Corinthains 8:12.

How exactly can we justify *"sinning against Christ"*?

IF it were actually Jesus that you were gossiping about would you still do it?

IF it was the Son of God would you still speak evil towards Him?

What it the Lord Jesus was to appear in the place of those who have been harassed, mocked, despised, rejected and belittled?

When a person in church is seen as a lesser being by the ruling elite do they ever think that they are actually sinning against Jesus Himself by behaving like that?

"If a man wearing a gold ring and fine clothing comes into your assembly, and a poor man in shabby clothing also comes in, and if you pay attention to the one who wears the fine clothing and say, "You sit here in a good place," while you say to the poor man, "You stand over there," or, "Sit down at my feet," have you not then made distinctions among yourselves and become judges with evil thoughts?" **James 2:2-4**

What James is condemning happens all too often in churches. When we make distinctions about people we are sinning and have wrong motives.

Let a banker come into our service and the congregation and leadership perks up and tries to put on their best show. I truly believe that it grieves the Spirit of God. But let an obviously poor family come in and many times they are treated just politely, but nobody worries about what they think or feel.

The banker will usually receive follow-up phone calls and letters and probably a visit from the senior pastor, but the poor family is lucky to get a letter. When people control us that much we are serving man and not God. One of the things that was abundantly clear about the Lord Jesus was that He showed no preference to anyone. He didn't care if they were poor, or what sex they were, or if they were famous. He treated all people the same.

Look at what James says in verse four: *"When you do this, when you make these kinds of distinctions, you have become judges with evil thoughts."*

What evil thoughts? Well, here's how you see that self-serving discrimination based on shallow externals. In the case of the rich man, when he arrives at the door and everybody goes, *"Boy, could he be a big giver to the congregation. No more budget troubles here. Come on, we've got a seat right up front for you."*

Whereas, when they see the poor person, the response is contempt. We wouldn't want a person like that, that bag lady, that tramp, that person from the wrong side of the tracks, we wouldn't want a person like that in our fellowship. We don't want our children to play with his children. We have a disdain for that person.

We forget where God found us when we allow ourselves to think higher of people based on external qualifications. God doesn't think that way and we had better be happy that He doesn't!

God went out of His way to make sure that the children of Israel didn't misunderstand why He chose them.

He said to them in **Deuteronomy 7:7** *"I did not set My love on you or choose you because you were more in number than any of the peoples. For you were the fewest of all peoples. But because I loved you and kept the oath which I swore to your forefathers."*

In other words He said; *"**The reason that you are Mine resides in Me, not in you.** I didn't look at you and count you worthy. I looked at you and I loved you just because I loved you. And therefore, I made you My own. And you are to treat others with that same spirit of mercy."*

The impact a person can have on a church is not measured by the amount of money they can put in the offering! I would rather have a praying grandmother than to have a self-serving millionaire.

Be careful how you judge people, because that is exactly how you are going to be judged! If we make a person feel unwelcome in our church we are forgetting that to that person we represent Jesus! We might be the only Jesus they ever meet—so be like Jesus.

Remember, *when we harm another believer we are sinning against Christ.*

Jesus sees what we do, He is hurt and grieved by our carelessness and indifference to the suffering we have caused another person. It should scare us!!!

When a child is molested, or someone is destroyed by careless and thoughtless words do we ever consider that Jesus feels that pain?

Beloved if you want to know what the Spirit feels when we harm another Christian just read what He had Paul write to the church at Corinth;

"Who is weak without my feeling that weakness? Who is led astray, and I do not burn with anger?" **2 Corinthians 11:29**

Paul's spirit was grieved because the Holy Spirit was grieved!

Jesus feels anger at seeing one of the little ones that He died for being harmed and led astray! It grieves His Spirit.

WHAT IF Jesus was to appear before us <u>and He was to bear on His body all of the wounds we have inflicted on others?</u>

That would cause every one of us to repent!

I know that many people believe that once they got saved they never have to repent again, but that is not true.

The reason why I bring this up is because many people believe that their sins are forgiven—past, present and future! So they can do anything that they want and never apologize or repent for it!

But is that what the bible teaches?

There have been times where people have actually tried to justify their misdeeds towards another believer by attempting to "*prove*" that person wasn't a good Christian. When you resort to doing that you are the one who isn't being a good Christian.

Many pastors weep for those who are driven out of their church by a fellow church member. Unfortunately they are often afraid to confront the devil disguised as a Christian who is running the people out of the church.

One of my mentors was Pastor Marvin Gorman.

In his church he had a family that had run the church for years before he arrived to pastor it. No matter what the pastor, congregation or the Holy Spirit wanted to do, that family had the final say.

One particular deacon was constantly causing trouble, but because he and his family ran the board there wasn't much Br. Gorman could do to remove him. That deacon would either have his way or he would make people leave.

Mercifully the church finally was able to grow enough that Br. Gorman could get some good men on the board to out-vote that deacon and his family.

When that happened they left the church.

Years later that old deacon lay dying in a hospital and he had his wife call Br. Gorman to please come pray with him.

With tears streaming down his face he asked Pastor Gorman to please forgive him for all the mean things that he had done.

Br. Gorman took him by the hand and with tears in his eyes he said to him, *"I forgave you when it happened. But now you must face Jesus and He is going to make you explain to Him why you insisted on running all of those good people out of church! You are going to have to answer for every soul that you sent to hell."*

The man's eyes bulged out in shock at Pastor's words, but he knew it was true.

That man waited until he was sure that he was dying before he could bring himself to apologize. It is doubtful that he meant it or he would have done it sooner. I fear for people like that when they meet their Maker.

Have no doubt about friend, Jesus is an honest Judge. He demands that we give an accounting of our lives and what we have done.

If there is sin in our life we should deal with it. If it is against a fellow believer we had better make it right.

"All wrongdoing is sin!" according to the apostle John in 1John 5:17. Any person who walks honestly with the Lord will have many occasions to repent of their sins.

Yet one of the worst sins is when we sin against another brother or sister in the Lord.

Jesus warned us that we would be better off being tied to a millstone and drown in the deepest sea as to destroy a brother or sister in Christ.

If the Lord was so adamant about that then how do you think He feels when we skandalize one of His people? And then we try to take Him by the hand and walk with Him!

The apostle's all taught that Christians who sinned had to repent if they sinned.

The apostle Paul spent a great deal of time and ink writing to the church at Corinth over their sinfulness. His desire was for them to repent. Why would he have done that if your sins are forgiven before you even commit them? No, Paul demanded that if a person sinned that they immediately repent of that sin.

What was the result of Paul's efforts?

*"Now I rejoice, not that you were grieved, **but that you grieved to repentance.** For you were grieved according to God, so that you might suffer loss by nothing in us. **For the grief according to God works repentance to salvation**, not to be regretted, but the grief of the world works out death."* 2 Corinthians 7:9-10

If it was God's desire to make the Christians repent then how can we teach them that they don't need to after their initial salvation experience?

And there were some who refused to repent, so to those people Paul sent this warning;

"For I fear, lest somehow coming I might not find you as I wish, and that I shall be found by you such as you might not wish; lest somehow there be strifes, envyings, angers, contentions, backbiting's, whisperings, proud thoughts, tumults; lest in my coming again my God will humble me with you; and I shall mourn many who have already sinned, and have not repented over the uncleanness, and fornication, and lustfulness which they have practiced." 2Corinthians 12:20-21

Clearly their lack of repentance was not going to be tolerated by the apostle!

So to those who have skandalized another person and don't believe that they owe that person an apology the bible says that they do!

And may I remind you that you are forgiven for those sins ***that you actually repent of***?!

If you refuse to give Jesus your whole heart then there are sins that ***He hasn't been able to forgive*** <u>because you haven't given them to Him.</u>

Jesus can and will forgive every sin that we give to Him and repent of. If we refuse to repent He simply can't forgive. We have a free will. He will allow us to live in sin if that is what we want.

We must confess our sins.

The apostle John was very clear;

*"If we say we have no sin, we deceive ourselves, and the truth is not in us. **If we confess our sins**, he is faithful and just to forgive us our sins and to cleanse us from all unrighteousness. If we say we have not sinned, we make him a liar, and his word is not in us."* <u>1John 1:8-10</u>

<u>***If we confess our sins!***</u> That is repentance!

Beloved, we do not have a choice if we want all of God in our lives! It is about relationships! Our relationship with God directly is linked to how we treat people. If we treat them like trash then don't expect God to treat you like a diamond!

If we have hurt someone we must seek reconciliation with that person if at all possible!

"If you are offering your gift at the altar and there remember that your brother has something against you, leave your gift there before the altar and go. First be reconciled to your brother, and then come and offer your gift." Matthew 5:23-24

I am a firm believer that many of our prayers go unanswered because we refuse to do this simple thing that the Lord commanded us to do.

Beloved, it takes a great deal of courage and an even greater amount of love to go and apologize for hurting a person.

There is an old saying that **"Only brave men apologize, cowards don't know how!"** And it is so true.

But if you do not repent and apologize you run the risk of destroying a person that Christ died to save!

"Do not destroy the one for whom Christ died!" Romans 14:15.

The original word translated as **destroy** actually means *"to put out of the way entirely, abolish, put an end to, to ruin."*

You can destroy a fellow Christian by your actions, and when you do you are sinning against Christ Himself!

It would be no different than if you were the one who drove the nails through His hands!

It is as if you hit Jesus repeatedly over His head with the rod.

How would you feel if you were the person who made Jesus the crown of thorns and shoved it down upon His brow?

Wouldn't your heart ache to think that you had hurt the Savior?

If so then don't hurt Him by hurting His people!

If you see Jesus instead of the person that you are about to gossip about or mistreat you might think twice about following through on your actions.

You wouldn't knowingly hurt Christ would you?

Yet many people do just that when they savage and attack other Christians.

Some might think, *"Well, I'm not convinced that they are Christians!"*

To those the Word of God says this; *"Who are you to pass judgment on the servant of another? It is before his own master that he stands or falls. And he will be upheld, for the Lord is able to make him stand."* Romans 14:4.

I do not agree with some people, especially those who behave like con-artist on TV, trying to make the Gospel a means of making money, but I will let God take care of them. It is not my job and personally I don't want to be their judge.

Remember—*it is about your relationship with Christ!*

"How can two walk together except they be in agreement?" Amos 3:3.

It seems to me that our relationship with Christ is the most essential relationship we can have, and if we damage that relationship we must repair it immediately.

If I offend Christ by harming my fellow believers then I must restore my relationship with Jesus at all costs!

If it cost me my pride so be it!

If it cost me shame so be it!

If it cost me status, prestige or anything else I must pay that price!

Apart from Jesus we can do NOTHING! We can accomplish NOTHING! Apart from Him we are NOTHING! So we cannot allow anything to separate us from Him.

Jesus said, *"If you love Me you will keep my commandments!"* in John 14:15.

Two of His commandments are that we love each other and that we love God.

The apostle's took those commandments to heart.

"If anyone says, "I love God," but hates his brother, he is a liar. For anyone who does not love his brother, whom he has seen, cannot love God, whom he has not seen." **1 John 4:20**

It is doubtful that anyone who blatantly and maliciously harms fellow Christians actually has a good relationship with God.

I realize that judging is not our job, but **Jesus said we would know them by their fruits**.

"Beware of false prophets, who come to you in sheep's clothing but inwardly are ravenous wolves. **You will recognize them by their fruits**. Are grapes gathered from thorn bushes, or figs from thistles? So, every healthy tree bears good fruit, but <u>**the diseased tree bears bad fruit.**</u>

A healthy tree cannot bear bad fruit, <u>**nor can a diseased tree bear good fruit.**</u> Every tree that does not bear good fruit is cut down and thrown into the fire. **Thus you will recognize them by their fruits**." Matthew 7:15-20

If they are persistently doing evil then they are evil.

You will know them by watching what fruit they produce.

A good tree CANNOT produce bad fruit according to the Lord Jesus!

Neither can a bad tree produce good fruit!

A bad tree always produces bad fruit—it is inevitable.

Many times people have been helped by family, friends and the church only to turn against the very ones who loved them.

One particular man was in need of groceries, so the pastor took him a carload one Sunday between services.

Did that man remember the good deed?

No, the last time he was at church he mocked the very people who had supplied his family with food.

No gratitude at all!

It is not uncommon. I wish it was. It is very common today for people to savage those who have helped them.

Have you ever wondered why people turn against you after you have helped them?

I will tell you why; they feel beholden to you after you help them and it makes them feel guilty. So instead of being gracious and thankful they become bitter and resentful. It is easier to tear down a good person than it is to feel indebted, so they tear you down.

The worse that they make you look the less they feel they owe you anything.

Have you ever been wounded by friends like those?

I think we all have.

When you realized that those people that you loved and trusted didn't love you but instead acted as if they hated you it hurt. We would be lying if we said that it didn't.

But *"friends"* means *"those who love Me!"* right?

Just because you are friends with someone does not necessarily mean that they are friends with you.

Watch people. If they are always trying to build up others, if their heart aches to see a person fall away from God, if they long for the presence of Almighty God at any price **they will bring forth good fruit.**

If however they are always backbiting and gossiping, causing trouble or helping to make a small problem into a big one **they will produce rotten and bad fruit.**

Most of the problems that have driven people from church originated with problem people.

They come down on anyone who dares to get in their way unsympathetically and hard. Soon they have bullied out of the church all who do not fit into their image of what a Christian should be.

And if along the way they drive out countless of hurting people so be it! The lost souls of others do not bother them at all!

All of this is going to be laid at the feet of the leadership of the church!

If they knowingly allow bullies to take advantage of God's people they are as guilty as the bully.

If they allow individuals to harm the flock and will not restrain them they are actually partaking in their crimes.

If they refuse to get involved for fear of repercussions it is proof positive that they fear men more than God.

The church must have strong leaders who fear God's wrath much more than they fear a local devil getting mad.

If a man or woman is allowed to rule the church by virtue of their anger or potential to cause trouble then SOMEONE is going to have to stop them even if it does get very unpleasant.

I speak from experience! It is never easy to uproot the devil's crowd—**but the church should belong to God and be run by the Holy Spirit!** We cannot allow the devil to manipulate the church through bullies, emotions or tantrums!

The devil will always organize a hit-squad that will react with fire and anger when anyone dares to stand up against them and what they are doing. We must be ready for it. But the stakes are too high to allow the devil to win! If he wins then people lose.

Leaders must lead! Or at least get out of the way and let an adult lead who is not afraid of people!

Beloved we are speaking of doing the Lord's work. Leaders who love the Lord Jesus will love and cherish the Lord's people. They will tend the flock that God has given to them.

And they will occasionally have to fight for the flock!

Sometimes the position of pastor requires that we use the rod and staff of a shepherd to drive away wolves. If we are not ready to do that then we had better pray that God gives us spines of steel so that we can.

"But you, dress yourself for work; arise, and say to them everything that I command you. Do not be dismayed by them, lest I dismay you before them. And I, behold, I make you this day a fortified city, an iron pillar, and bronze walls, against the whole land, against the kings of Judah, its officials, its priests, and the people of the land. They will fight against you, but they shall not prevail against you, for I am with you, declares the LORD, to deliver you." Jeremiah 1:17-19

God told Jeremiah ahead of time that he was going to face much adversity and it still almost overwhelmed him.

In the end God kept Jeremiah from being destroyed, but He brought down everyone who opposed Jeremiah's message.

God would not have put people in positions of leadership if He didn't believe that they could get the job done! So if you are a leader stand up and be an adult and lead in the fear of the Lord.

Jesus told us that we too would face adversity and persecution if we take a stand alongside of Him.

Should we expect anything different from the enemy?

It is time to take the mantle back and put it squarely on our shoulders again and do the Lord's work!

Perhaps you are a victim of the devil's hit squad?

One of his people singled you out for persecution or destruction and you were wounded deeply.

What do you do now?

What does the Lord want you to do?

In the next part of this book we will deal with how to get free from the devil's bondage in your life.

Chapter 5: Trust the Lord with judgement!

> *"We must learn to regard people less in the light of what they do or omit to do, and more in the light of what they suffer."* — **Dietrich Bonhoeffer**

Our first response to betrayal is often anger. The frustration and hurt within us makes us want to fight back. We might try to get even with those who have hurt us, or to go around *"setting the record straight"* but that never works. All that does is to keep the turmoil going longer than it should have.

Jesus gave us the proper example of how to handle betrayal.

When you read in the Book of Hebrews about how Jesus suffered, and feared, and wept in chapter 5:7-8 we must put ourselves in His place. If that were one of us we also would have been scared! We would have suffered knowing what was happening and what was about to happen to us! I know I would have wept too!

Yet in all of that Jesus never sinned! Never!

I doubt if any of us could endure what He endured without sinning.

He continued on to the assignment that he was commissioned to by the Father.

Though Jesus' internal struggle with Judas' betrayal is not recorded, we can assume that it was difficult for Him. Jesus instructed Judas to do what he'd set his mind to. He didn't stop him or throw a fit. Jesus responded to Judas graciously even though He knew what Judas, His *"friend"* was about to do!

Jesus responded to Judas' betrayal with kindness and grace.

If we have been betrayed by someone close to us—and eventually we all will—our first response should be to cry out to Jesus who loves us, pursues us, and intimately understands the reality of that betrayal.

One of the hardest things to get people to turn loose of after they have been wounded is the feeling of vengeance. They demand justice, and justice seldom is swift.

God knows more about our situation than we do. So we must leave things like retribution and revenge in His hands. We only want judgment; **_but God wants righteous judgment._**

We are not aware of the true nature of the world around us. Not really. There are myriads of wounded souls who walk by us every day and we cannot recognize their hurts because they hide them so well. But God knows.

A man who was mistreated his whole life turned out to be an abusive husband and father. Once we find out his backstory we will have some compassion towards him. But God already knew his backstory! God hasn't allowed him to die for a reason!

If you found out that the mean-spirited woman who can't say anything nice about anyone suffered terribly as a child, does that change how you view her? Can you find compassion for her now that we now how she has suffered?

My point is that often there are complicating circumstances behind the actions of others.

THAT DOESN'T EXCUSE IT! But perhaps it will help us to pray for that person where before we might not have.

We have to keep in mind that not everyone that we run into acts bad on purpose. Some have been pushed into behaving that way, so cut them some slack and pray for them.

That doesn't mean to imply that they get off scot-free! But I suspect that God has more leniency with them than we tend to do.

Have you ever considered that Jesus wants to save the worst people you know?

I mean even those people who have hurt us!

Jesus wanted to save the people that He knew beforehand were going to kill Him!

In the Gospel of Mark there is the remarkable story of Jesus healing a man with a withered hand on the Sabbath.

Although He did not break the Sabbath according to the Law of Moses, the Pharisees condemned Him for breaking their rules for the Holy Day.

*"Again he entered the synagogue, and a man was there with a withered hand. And they watched Jesus, to see whether he would heal him on the Sabbath, so that they might accuse him. And he said to the man with the withered hand, "Come here." And he said to them, "Is it lawful on the Sabbath to do good or to do harm, to save life or to kill?" But they were silent. And **he looked around at them with anger, grieved at their hardness of heart**, and said to the man, "Stretch out your hand." He stretched it out, and his hand was restored. The Pharisees went out and immediately held counsel with the Herodians against him, how to destroy him."* Mark 3:1-6

Anger is the translation of the Greek word *"Or-gay"* which means *"to be deeply stirred in your emotions."* In other words, Jesus' emotions were visible—it moved Him greatly to see how lost the Pharisees were. The second word that I want you to pay attention to is the word translated as **grieved**. It is the Greek word *"sullupeo."* It means *"to cause great grief."* Jesus was deeply, emotionally moved when He saw how hard and unrepentant the Jewish leaders were. It grieved Him! He felt sorrow—grief, for their lostness!

Picture this scene in your mind's eye; Jesus looks at the lost leaders and His sympathies are aroused in Him as He looks at them. They have no sympathy for Jesus or the lame man, but Jesus had sympathy for them, for He knew better than anyone what fate awaited them if they refused to repent.

We must remember the heart of God the Father was expressed in Jesus Christ. There was no difference between Father and Son when it came to compassion for the lost— **all of the lost!**

"For God so loved <u>the world</u> that He gave His only-begotten Son, that whoever believes in Him should not perish but have everlasting life. For God did not send His Son into <u>the world</u> to condemn <u>the world</u>, but so that <u>the world</u> might be saved through Him." <u>John 3:16-17</u>

That is the heart of God the Father! He desires to save EVERYONE in the world!

Even those people that we deem unworthy of His mercies are people that God loves and wants to save!

Everyone on planet earth needs Jesus! Every single one!

In the Book of Ecclesiastes, written by Solomon when he was very old, there is this unusual verse;

"I saw all the oppressions that are done under the sun. And behold, the tears of the oppressed, and <u>they had no one to comfort them!</u> On the side of their oppressors there was power, and <u>there was no one to comfort them.</u>" <u>Ecclesiastes 4:1.</u>

This verse has proven troublesome to interpreters for centuries because the way it reads is that the oppressed and the oppressors all lack comfort when they need it.

Our view of right and wrong makes us only take the side of the poor oppressed people, *<u>but God loves everyone</u>*— even the bad ones!

It might shake our preconceived ideas of God to find out that He also loves those who have harmed us. Just because we have consigned them to hell forever doesn't mean that God has.

Consider the apostle Paul; he murdered many Christian men and women! See Acts 8:1-3 & 9:1.

Have you ever considered the families of those innocent people? Did Saul—Paul—make them orphans? What happened to them after he was done wrecking their lives?

I'm sure if you had inquired of them whether or not they thought Saul of Tarsus was worth saving they would have had a hard time saying that he was.

Yet God loved Saul of Tarsus and through an encounter with the resurrected Savior he became the apostle Paul and the Gospel of Jesus Christ's greatest champion.

My point is that we tend to be guilty of assuming that God thinks what we think and feels what we feel, so if we don't like someone we assume that He naturally feels like we do. Well it isn't true! God loves sinners! All of them!

Beloved the reason why you should forgive people is so that God can be free to do His best work in you. It is hard to forgive that monster that destroyed your life—I know! *But for your sake* you simply have no choice.

You don't forgive people so that they will change because they may never change.

There are some people who refuse to change. They will not alter their behavior no matter how many scriptures you give to them or how kind you treat them.

What do we do with people who refuse to be nice? We show them mercy anyway! That's exactly what we are commanded to do. Then we leave those people to God! He will do all that He can to save them, but ultimately it is between those people and God. Once we forgive them there is nothing more we can do except to pray for them.

You do not have to bring them back into your circle. You do not have to even associate with them. But you MUST forgive them.

After you have forgiven someone you pray for them and let God have them. Releasing them into God's merciful hands is the best thing you can do for yourself and those who despitefully use you.

But I say unto you, Love your enemies, bless them that curse you, do good to them that hate you, and pray for them which despitefully use you, and persecute you; That ye may be the children of your Father which is in heaven. Matthew 5:44-45

If you desire God's blessings then you have to keep God's commandments to "Love your enemies!"

We have to bless those who curse us!

We should be looking for ways to do good to them that hate us!

And above all—we are to pray for them!

I realize that we desire to see a change take place when we pray for people, but it doesn't always happen the way we prefer.

We pray for the ones who have hurt us for our sake as well as theirs. Our prayers for those who treat us wrong should serve to change our hearts and minds. We ought to reap the benefits of sowing mercy into their lives by becoming more merciful.

But someone will undoubtedly ask the question of "what happens if they treat me worse instead?"

That is when we leave them in God's hands and stand away from them. But we still have to pray for them. There are some people that are so toxic that a saint can't stay in their presence very long.

The Lord Jesus faced some people like that. He told the disciples to *"Leave them alone! They are blind leaders of the blind!"* Matthew 15:14.

Some people are past redeeming. They wouldn't accept God's help if He came to them personally.

Let's face it, some people are just mean. They were mean from childhood for no good reason and they haven't mellowed with age! We must always pray for everyone, but we cannot save them, only God can. ***If they do not want to change we can't make them!***

In the books of **Exodus** and **Numbers** we read how the children of Israel quickly turned away from God and made a golden calf.

It took all of 40 days for them to go from praising and worshipping God as He spoke to them to bowing down to an idol that they had made!

God was so angry that He wanted to wipe out the entire nation and start over with Moses!

Moses interceded and begged God to forgive the people.

In the end God spared them *for a while,* but He promised them that their bodies would fall in the Wilderness during a 40 year forced march.

"For indeed the hand of the LORD was against them, to destroy them from among the host, until they were consumed." Deuteronomy 2:15

In other words, **there were some people that not even God could change.**

If you read the book of Romans 1:24-32 you will find the phrase *"God gave them up"* repeated three times. When a people push God too far He will give them the desires of their hearts even though He knows it will destroy them.

Dr. Donald Grey Barnhouse called this the most terrible passage in the entire Bible. That in itself is a remarkable claim, considering how much of the Bible deals with judgment on the sin of mankind. But I believe Dr. Barnhouse is correct. This is the most terrible, most awesome, most shocking passage in the entire Bible.

Consider the impact of these verses;

Verse 24 — *"God gave them up"*

Verse 26 — *"God gave them up"*

Verse 28 — *"He gave them up"*

The word in Greek is ***paredoken***.

The King James translates it as *"God gave them up."*

Barclay renders it *"God abandoned them."*

J. B. Phillips says, *"They gave up God. So God gave them up."*

It is a very strong word, meaning that act of God whereby he hands over the human race for judgment because of their sins.

In this passage Paul is telling us what happens when men turn away from God. *"When men lose God, they always lose themselves."*

It's as if God has said, *"All right. If you want to turn away from me, I'll let you go. I won't try to stop you. But you'll have to face the consequences of your own actions."*

If people refuse to surrender their lives to God He will honor their choice.

If God can't make everyone love Him then neither can we. If God Almighty can't cause people to behave then neither can we.

The point beloved is that we must not fall into the trap of being men pleasers because that is something that even God can't do.

Someone once said that *"Man is a terrible and cruel taskmaster"* meaning that once you submit to a person and allow them to rule over you, you will find it is impossible to please them.

It is due to our own vanity and pride that we think we can make people like us. Not even the Lord Jesus could accomplish that! So who are we to think we can?

When we worry about what people think of us we are bowing down to them, not God.

That is not to say that we shouldn't care about people's feelings, we should. But we cannot let their feelings overrule us from doing what we know is right. <u>*If God said it we must do it*</u> regardless of who agrees or disagrees.

We judge according to what we see and feel, but God judges according to what that person is in their heart. He sees the unseen.

We must recognize that we can't guarantee who is willing to change so we had better leave that to God. We are to love the unlovable, and until God says differently we had better keep doing what we are doing.

You can be sure that one day the sinners will be punished far worse than any court among men can punish them. There is no prison system on earth that can equal the torments of hell.

It is the feeling that somebody is *"getting away with it"* that fuels much of our anger. We have all been hurt by someone, only to see them going on with their lives, apparently unpunished.

Let me warn you against judging by the eyes, you can be deceived. I have lived long enough to see the end of many arrogant and abusive people. God always gets the last word! Always!

I have seen the children of those hypocrites leave home and never go to church because of everything that they witnessed at home. They reap the bad seeds that they have sown in their own households!

Their children are often the beneficiaries of their actions, and it is not fair to the kids. They didn't cause their parents to act badly.

If you could see everything that their actions brought on their lives and those that they love you would not be clamoring for revenge. You may even pray for mercy.

I know that may seem unlikely to you if you have been abused, but in time God may let you see what has happened to them and you might change your mind.

When we are hurt we want immediate justice, and often that doesn't happen.

This is a cruel and twisted world that we live in, and bad things often happen to good people for no apparent reason.

We expect that sinners will hurt us sometimes, but what about when so-called saints hurt us? How do we deal with them?

Let me remind you that every saint is a human being who also fights against his sinful nature every moment of every day of his life. Sometimes they fail to keep their sin nature at bay.

Again, this is not excusing their behavior at all. It is just a way of saying that God knows and He will deal with it, so let Him be God.

Let God be God over all of your life, even the parts that hurt. He will deal honestly and fairly and He will show mercy.

Be certain of this—the Lord will judge everyone! The righteous and the sinner will all face the same God.

The Lord will judge His people! Hebrews 10:30

"For it is time for judgment to begin at the household of God; and if it begins with us, what will be the outcome for those who do not obey the gospel of God? If the righteous is scarcely saved, what will become of the ungodly and the sinner?" 1 Peter 4:17-18

Before we demand justice for others we had better think about what would happen to us if God judged us according to our works and not according to His mercy!

We are not saved by our righteousness, because it is like a filthy rag or an unclean thing to God. We are saved by faith in the risen Savior and what He did on Calvary's cross in our place. We call that mercy.

A Christian ought to show more mercy than anyone else on earth! He ought to, but not everyone who claims to know the Lord personally actually does. Some are pretend Christians who love to act religious, but have never surrendered their lives to God.

They are the people who often do us the most damage because we allow them to get close to us because we truly believe that they love God and us.

The Lord Jesus warned us that we would have to endure persecutions and torture for His name's sake, but He never meant that we would also have to be skandalized by church members.

When a friend hurts us with the result being that we are turned away from Jesus and turned off from church that person has not just wounded us—they have sinned against Jesus. He definitely takes that personally!

We are His body on earth—flesh of His flesh and bone of His bone. Read Ephesians 5:21-32 and you will see that Jesus considers the church to be His bride. We belong to Him.

As the husband loves his wife as if she were his own flesh even so does our heavenly Groom love us.

The Lord Jesus said, *"Woe to the world because of offenses! For it is necessary that offenses come; but woe to that man by whom the offense comes!"* Matthew 18:7.

Woe means *"danger! Be cautious! Watch out!"*

Jesus is warning that anyone who harms one of His little ones had better be cautious, because they are in grave danger!

"Take heed that ye despise not one of these little ones; for I say unto you, That in heaven their angels do always behold the face of my Father which is in heaven." Matthew 18:10

What did Jesus mean by *"In heaven their angels do always behold the face of My Father"*?

Simply that they report directly to God all that they see.

No matter how that wicked person may justify what they have done to you, the angels saw it first hand and they know the unvarnished truth.

When that person is forced to face the Righteous Judge he may try to justify himself, but there will be an angel standing there who saw it for himself. He will tell the truth.

So let God judge and you remember to trust His judgment. When we do that the peace of God will help us get through the hurt.

Remember—if you are going to be God and administer judgment then you are going to have to do all of the God-stuff! That means that you will have to heal yourself, console yourself and do everything else that you need.

It is so much simpler to let God be God!

The apostle Paul wrote to the Christians saying, *"If it is possible on your part, live at peace with everyone. Do not avenge yourselves, beloved, but leave room for God's wrath. For it is written: "Vengeance is Mine; I will repay, says the Lord." On the contrary, "If your enemy is hungry, feed him; if he is thirsty, give him a drink. For in so doing, you will heap burning coals on his head."* Romans 12:18-20.

Now remember that these were terrible times to be a Christian in Rome!

Nero was wrapping them in oil-soaked blankets and setting them on fire to light his garden at night!

They were being treated horribly!

And Paul knew that things were about to get a whole lot worse!

So what was Paul's advice?

Leave the vengeance and wrath to God.

God can be trusted to avenge His children!

The Lord Jesus said, *"Will not God bring about justice for His elect who cry out to Him day and night? Will He continue to delay their help? I tell you, He will promptly carry out justice on their behalf."* Luke 18:7-8

When we let go is when God can take control. He is not going to wrestle you for control! You and I must surrender to His controlling hand.

It hurts. It hurts thinking about being betrayed because it brings it all back—all of the hurts, all of the betrayal of trust, all of the feeling of having your heart broken-*it hurts!*

I understand. Your hurt may be worse than any others, but there are some things that you must do if you really want to be free.

Hear me please—*what you do with your hurt is perhaps more important than the hurt itself.*

It will either define you or *you will allow God to define you*—but it can't be both ways. One or the other will define who you are.

Will you be a victim all of your life or a victor?

Would you prefer to get back to living your life?

Or do you prefer to reflect unceasingly about the past and something that cannot be changed?

How do you let go of past hurts and move on? Can you? Will you?

In the book "**Cradles of Innocence**" *by Victor and Mildred Goertzel* they studied over 700 successful people from various fields.

They wanted to see if there was a correlation between their childhoods and their later success in life. To their great surprise most of the people did not come from easy backgrounds.

On the contrary they tended to come from troubled homes, troubled lives or they suffered some form of disability.

While no one wants to suffer, it often is the force that drives people to push further, try harder and not accept defeat. Without obstacles they would never have succeeded to the level that they did!

They reported that *"three-fourths of the children are troubled-by poverty, a broken home, rejection, over possessive, estranged, or dominating parents; by financial ups and downs; by physical handicaps, or by parental dissatisfaction with the children's school failures."* **Chapter 11—Out of the Cradle Endlessly Rocking, pages 281-283.**

Handicaps such as blindness, deafness, being crippled, sickly, homely, undersized, and overweight or a speech defect occurred in one-fourth of the people as children.

Yet rather than holding them back their handicaps actually helped instill in them the determination to overcome and gave them their drive to succeed.

It is simply amazing how many people with past hurts achieved great things, not by denying their hurts but by using them and turning their greatest weakness into their greatest strength. They got used to overcoming! It became their new normal!

We must always remember that we are not alone in what we suffer.

Many people have survived what we suffered from and we can too. But how did they turn the hurt into a strength?

Every single successful person <u>had to change their thinking first.</u>

There came a point in their lives where they stopped allowing their handicap to define them. They stopped making excuses why they couldn't do things and started looking at ways that they could accomplish their goals.

It was a new mindset that they achieved before they achieved success.

Beloved, losing can become easy! Winning can seem too hard. But a loser can become a winner simply by not accepting defeat. When we accept losing as our normal we are denying the Word of God over our lives.

We tend to give people a pass on their bad behavior if we find out that they have been really hurt. It is an automatic assumption on our part that hurting people tend to act out their frustrations and their hurts in ways that are not always pleasant.

But we expect that they will stop hurting others and behaving badly after they have had time to heal.

What I am talking about all of us have come in contact with and that is a person with a martyr complex who refuses to get out of their self-imposed pity box.

I am not belittling their suffering, but sooner or later they must get out of the pit and start achieving something or else they will waste their God-given mandate for their life! God gives all of us tasks to accomplish and He believes that with His help everyone can achieve something worthwhile.

The thing about our souls being wounded is that the scars are not visible but the pain is. It shows up in every area of our lives.

We can try to make everyone "see" how hurt we are by constantly talking about it but that never brings us healing. The feeling of comfort we get from others only last for a few minutes. Inevitably they will tire of hearing the same old stories and they will start avoiding us if we keep acting that way.

The point is that we cannot allow ourselves to live in that place of hurt and torment!

We want to blame the perpetrator and let everyone know what a scoundrel they are. We want them punished and we want everyone to see them for what they really are.

However the danger in doing that is that we tend to LIVE IN our hurts and vengeance. It fills our hearts and souls until there is no room for anything else.

That person has taken over our lives!

The wrong that they did to us has come to define us.

You may be thinking, *"But they ought to have to answer for what they did!"*

True, and if there is a legal remedy then use it.

However even then you will have to let it go eventually.

A man who molested his children and grandchildren lived to be a ripe old age. That alone didn't seem fair. He had gotten away with ruining the lives of his daughters and their children. He had set their lives on a destructive course. And he lived to be an old man! That doesn't seem fair, I know.

But he died without Jesus and he is suffering untold horrors in hell today. **<u>NOTHING</u> on this earth can compare to the terrors that he endures endlessly**, and will endure forever.

<u>BUT!</u> Where were the other adults during the times that he was molesting his children? Why did any of his adult daughters allow their daughters within a hundred miles of that old pervert?

God put people and institutions in place to deal with men like that, but adults have to be adults and take charge. Somebody, usually the wife, turned a blind eye and allowed the abuse to continue.

If we allow ourselves to we can stay in that place of torment and aggravation forever. There is no end of the things we can find to be mad or hurt about. But we accomplish nothing by staying there!

We might think that we are only in that place because someone did something awful to us. Perhaps that is right! But you are not supposed to stay in the pit if you are a Christian! Get up, get going and do something!

Blaming others for our hurt is what most of us start off doing. Somebody did something wrong, or they wronged us in some way that mattered to us.

We want them to apologize. We want them to acknowledge what they did was wrong.

The problem with blaming others is that it can often leave you powerless. Your life, your joy, your happiness is contingent on punishing the person who did you wrong.

What if you do confront them and they deny it? Or worse yet, they simply act as if it is no big deal?

That leaves you worse off because you still have your hurt and anger but there is no resolution.

All your feelings are legitimate. But they should have a time limit! Eventually they will stain your soul and cause you to become the very type of person you hate.

Harboring your grievances forever is a bad habit, because it hurts you more than it hurts them. They walked away! You are stuck where they hurt you.

The only way you can accept new joy and happiness into your life is to make room for it.

If your heart is filled to overflowing with pain and hurt, how can you have room for anything good that the Lord wants to give you?

Some people actually feel guilty if they laugh!

It is almost impossible for them to enjoy anything.

Why? Because their hurt defines them.

Let it go and give it to God!

"Cast all of your anxieties on him, because he cares for you." 1 Peter 5:7.

The original Greek word translated as *"anxieties"* is *"merimna"* which means *"**DISTRACTIONS.**"*

That is what they are—distractions. They keep us from enjoying the life that God wants us to have. We can become so bogged down that we stop looking up.

That is why we need to make the commitment to *"let it go and let God have it."*

By not letting go we sabotage our life and keep God from working in us.

He can only mold the clay that we give Him!

Beloved it is liberating to realize that we do have a choice whether to dwell permanently in our hurts or to move on and live. That doesn't mean we will forget what has happened, but it does mean that the person who hurt us no longer has any control over us.

As long as what they did controls our lives they actually do control us. We must stop letting them!

We stop reliving the past pain, and we stop going over the details of the story in our heads every time we think of the other person.

It is our choice to either hold on to the pain, or to live a life without it.

You can and should find someone you can trust to confide in. It should be a pastor or someone else who can be trusted to keep it private. It would do you a great deal of good to share what has happened to you.

But be warned; *not everyone is going to guard your heart and not everyone can be trusted.* Some will gossip and that will result in your pain being multiplied. So pray and seek God's guidance first.

If you have been victimized it is very easy to play the victim card. However it is not liberating! It is actually imprisonment for your soul.

Make up your mind that you will not be the victim anymore. Victimhood can give us the feeling that we are justified in our behavior, but it is never liberating. And ultimately we will see that there is no justification for us doing bad things just because we were hurt. *Hurting others because we were hurt is not something we can justify.*

We have a choice! We do! Will we continue to feel bad because of what some monster did to us or will we choose to start enjoying life?

Jesus said that He came so that we might have life—and an abundant life! John 10:10.

Decide that you are going to live that abundant life.

You have the power to choose. Do not let others choose for you!

Will you continue to stay stuck in your land of hurts and sorrow or will you give your hurts and sorrows to God?

The responsibility is yours.

Why would you let the person who hurt you — in the past — have such power, right here, right now?

No amount of thinking has ever fixed a relationship problem. Never. Not in the entirety of the world's history. So why choose to engage in so much thought and devote so much energy to a person who you feel has wronged you?

It is time to focus on the present. **_Today is your day!_**

"This is the day that the Lord has made! I will rejoice and be glad in it!" Psalm 118:24

Write your own story. Choose to not be the long-suffering martyr! Start being the heroic person who breaks free from their shackles and gets out of the prison house!

You can't undo the past, but you can make today the best day of your life!

As Christians we are to look at the world we live in TODAY.

We should not dwell in the past, it's over.

We can't get to worrying about tomorrow either! Jesus said, *"Therefore do not worry about tomorrow, for tomorrow will worry about itself. Each day has enough trouble of its own."* Matthew 6:34.

Fill your mind and heart with the good things of God and family and friends and you will have less room for the devil's junk.

Negative thinking crowds out positive thinking. Choose to be positive in your affirmation of yourself and others.

And—*forgive them*. Not because they deserve it!

Forgive them because you need it!

We always expect God and others to forgive us, but many of us don't have it in our hearts to forgive others. But don't forget that an unforgiving heart knows nothing about happiness. It only dwells in bitterness and resentment. Not happiness.

Forgiving is not forgetting.

I once had a man who did me and my family very much harm. For years I tried everything to get along with him, but finally I realized that it wasn't going to happen.

After another of his famous fits of rage I informed him that we had had enough. Screaming insults at me he tried everything to get me to fight him, but I knew better than to take that bait. I stood my ground and he finally stormed off and our lives were better for it.

He had problems, issues that needed to be dealt with. But his actions precluded anyone from being able to reach him. He affected every area of the church—negatively. If he had his way we would have had only one sheep to tend and it would have been him. That simply is not right and cannot be tolerated.

One person cannot be allowed to destroy a church! There are many people there that God sent for the purpose of them being healed and helped.

If one wicked person so dominates the church that it is always in a state of turmoil God is not going to send any of His sheep to that place!

When that man was gone we had peace in our church and thanked God for it. Toxic people poison everything that they come in contact with. Sometimes we are just better off without them.

Years later he came to me and asked me to please forgive him. I replied that I had forgiven him a long time ago.

He smiled and said, *"Does that mean that we are friends again?"*

"No" I answered him, *"I forgave you, but I know I cannot trust you! I will continue to love you and pray for you, but I don't believe that we can ever have a close personal friendship because those are built on trust. You will have to earn my trust again."*

He got very angry and shouted at me, *"Well then you haven't forgiven me!"* Instantly he again flew into a fit of rage, confirming to me that he had not changed.

Indeed, I knew that he hadn't changed because I knew people who were in his inner circle. They were being harmed by him on a consistent basis—including his own wife and children.

He was trying to force me to do what he wanted, which was to let him back into our lives.

After so many years of enduring harm at his hands that wasn't going to happen. But I did forgive him. To this day I pray that God helps him.

But I would be a fool to allow that man back into my life.

We **do not have to forget** another person's bad behaviors, but for our own sakes **we must forgive** them.

Forgiveness isn't saying, *"I agree with what you did."* That has nothing to do with it! It is saying for my sake I choose to forgive you even if you refuse to accept it.

Remember that the Lord Jesus said, *"And whenever you stand praying, forgive, if you have anything against anyone, so that your Father also who is in heaven may forgive you your trespasses."* Mark 11:25.

IF we forgive we will be forgiven. IF we do not forgive then neither will we be forgiven.

Forgiveness isn't a sign of weakness. *It's a sign of strength.*

Remember, only brave men forgive! Cowards never do!

When you were wounded it put you on the path to destruction, and only you can get off of that path.

And please understand; the devil wants to destroy you!

For every struggle the enemy will be working on you to keep you from breaking free. He will whisper in your ears that it is not your fault that you act like you do.

There will always be a sliver of truth in what the devil says, but he will not tell the whole story.

It may not have been your fault—true! But you do not have to stay in the pit of torment one second longer! You can be free!

One lady surprised me after I had been teaching on this subject in church. As soon as the altar service was over she came up to me and told me this, *"My mother is no longer going to live in my head rent-free!"*

That's what happens when we allow grief, hurts and other things to take over our lives—we actually allow the perpetrators of our pain to control us.

This young lady finally saw this truth and it set her free.

She was now a grown woman with children and grandchildren of her own and her mother still controlled her—but no more.

She said that she finally saw what was going on and was going to put a stop to being manipulated by guilt and shame.

If we are ever to get free we are going to have to be totally honest with God.

Think of the blind man Bartimaeus; In Mark's Gospel 10:46-52 we read his story.

For many years he sat alongside the thoroughfare leading through Jericho begging for alms.

If you had walked by him any other day you would have seen a man comfortable with his situation. He was blind and he begged for money to help him survive.

But looks don't do the blind man justice! He accepted his situation but he never **really** accepted it! No! He wanted his two eyes to work! He wanted to be free from his dark world!

And then one day he heard a crowd approaching him. *"What is going on?"* he asked towards anyone who would listen.

"The prophet Jesus of Nazareth is coming by!" they answered him.

Jesus of Nazareth? Bartimaeus had heard plenty about Him! He healed the sick! He even raised the dead! This was Bartimaeus' one chance to change His life and he jumped at it.

He couldn't walk through the crowd but he could shout loud enough to be heard!

"Jesus, Son of David! Have mercy on me!!!" He yelled at the top of his lungs!

Friend that kind of determination will cause heaven to stop and listen to you!

Jesus could see from his clothing that he was blind for he wore the garments of a blind beggar. But Jesus wanted Bartimaeus to speak what he wanted!

"What do you want Me to do for you?" Jesus asked him.

With his heart beating rapidly from excitement and anticipation Bartimaeus chose his words carefully!

"Lord, that I might recover my sight!" he said.

And Jesus said to him, "Go your way; your faith has made you well." And immediately he recovered his sight and followed him on the way. Mark 10:52

Notice that Bartimaeus RECOVERED his sight!

He had been born with good eyes, but had lost his sight. The enemy took from him something precious. His whole life was changed when he lost his sight.

That had to have been traumatic to him, but he left the trauma behind and went towards Jesus! That is what we have to do.

"But Pastor" someone will say, *"What about justice? How come I don't get to watch them pay for what they did?"*

I counsel you to get as close to God as you possibly can and I assure you that you will hear His voice saying to you gently—*"Leave that person to Me!"*

And that is exactly what we must do.

The church in Corinth had many messes on their hands. Some of them were due to a lack of understanding and others were due to a lack of love.

They had church people in the Corinthian church who were defrauding others within the same church.

They were taking advantage of their brothers and sisters in Christ.

The ones who had been done wrong were filing lawsuits against the ones who had cheated them. It was getting ugly in the house of God.

Paul the apostle's advice was not what you would have expected though!

He said, *"To have lawsuits at all with one another is already a defeat for you. Why not rather suffer wrong? Why not rather be defrauded?"* 1 Corinthians 6:7.

He is not condoning the one who had cheated the others. In fact Paul demanded that they stop doing it and make amends. However his words were to those who had been hurt. He wanted them to let go and give it to God.

Paul had been a bitter and mean-spirited young man when Christ found him. He understood better than most the danger of allowing that root of bitterness to grow.

That is why Paul's advice was to let it go. It just isn't worth it to hang onto that hurt.

Remember;

"It is a fearful thing to fall into the hands of the living God." Hebrews 10:31.

Chapter 6: Imagination, friend or foe?

"I shut my eyes in order to see!" **Paul Gauguin**

God speaks to our hearts first, not our heads. The heart ***is the soul***. It is where our emotions and desires reside. If we will listen for God's voice as we pray and meditate upon His Word we will hear Him in our hearts.

It is in the heart that God implants dreams, visions and goals. He speaks to our spiritual ears words of encouragement and direction.

God speaks to you from His heart to your heart.

Literally it is from God's imagination to ours!

The power of your imagination is almost without limits. With your imagination you can fight wars, travel to the moon, rescue a child or even be a famous singer.

A healthy imagination is a blessing.

But your imagination can also become a prison!

If you only see the negative side of a situation you will wall yourself inside of a prison of your own making.

People who have suffered so long that it is all that they see can rarely break free from that place of darkness. It is the place where they are at home, so to speak. It is where they are comfortable, even though it is also a place of loneliness and misery.

William Blake wrote a poem about the power of the imagination called **"The Auguries of Innocence."** In it he describes the beauty and the danger of the imagination. It begins;

"To see a World in a Grain of sand
And a Heaven in a wild flower
Hold infinity in the palm of your hand
And Eternity in an hour"

It sounds beautiful. To open our imaginations to see the unseen is God's way.

To understand the handiwork of God in even the smallest of things is a great gift. If you can see God in everything around you it will help you to know that He surrounds you, He puts great planning and care into all of His decisions concerning you. And that He is intently interested in showing to you His great love and care.

But the poem takes a darker turn and ends this way;

"We are led to believe a lie
When we see not through the eye
Which was born in a night to perish in a night
When the soul slept in beams of light
God appears and God is light
To those poor souls who dwell in night
But does a human form display
To those who dwell in realms of day?"

In other words, although God shows up in our darkness **can we who are so used to darkness grasp the light**?

We sometimes become used to living in pity.

Let's face it, there is a certain pleasure in being pitied and the flesh loves it!

Who doesn't want attention?

Who doesn't want to be noticed, appreciated and made to feel special?

Yet all of that can become bound by the need for pity. It can become our prison and keep us from being free.

If you have been harmed it is normal to want to be comforted, but you cannot stay in the place where you receive constant pity!

Sooner or later you will have to stand back up and get back into life.

And **how you see yourself** and your situation has a powerful impact on your life.

If you believe that due to a trauma in your life you can never be happy again you won't be.

If you read in the bible that through Christ you can have a new life and that old things are passed away and you believe it applies to you, you will have a great life. If you believe that that means you can enjoy life again you will.

Really it is **<u>how you see yourself to be inwardly</u>** that determines much of your outward reality.

You might think, *"Well pastor, my reality is that I am broken and helpless!"*

That may be true—from a certain vantage point anyway.

<u>But from heaven's vantage point it may be completely untrue!</u>

How God sees you *is far more important than how anyone else sees you.*

Your imagination is based on supposed facts. *But what if you have your facts wrong?*

What if your imagination is faulty?

Paul J. Meyer wrote a short story called "**The Black Door.**" It gives great insight into human nature.

In the story a spy is captured during war. The warlord sentenced him to death. But he gives him the choice to either face a quick death by the firing squad or take his chances by passing through a mysterious black door.

Ominously he tells the spy that no one has ever come back who went through the door. Then he marched him into the courtyard and asked the frightened spy, *"What have you chosen: the firing squad or the black door?"*

The spy's imagination began to run wild! There might be lions or tigers behind that door. Or he might even be drawn and quartered! He had heard so many wild and frightening stories about this particular warlord that he shuddered to think of what might be on the other side of that big black door.

"I would rather die quickly than slowly!" the spy replied, *"I choose the firing squad!"* He was then placed against the wall and shot.

With an air of disgust the warlord turned to his aide and said, *"You see how it is with people? They will always prefer the known to the unknown. That man went quietly to his death though I gave him a choice."*

His aide stared at the door; he had never seen what was on the other side either.

"What lies beyond the black door?" asked the aide.

"Freedom," replied the warlord, *"and I've known very few men brave enough to take it."*

It was his imagination that killed the spy! He imagined that under no circumstances would he be allowed his freedom, so he never entertained the thought.

I have known countless people who are bound in prisons of their own making and **they cannot imagine being free, so it never enters their mind.**

Friend, you should be free in Christ!

You should have joy unspeakable and full of glory!

If you are not experiencing the goodness of God there is a reason, and it may have to do with your vision of your life.

It could be that you're imagining things not as they are but as they are not!

Albert Einstein said, *"Your imagination is your preview of life's coming attractions!"*

That is not only true in the positive; it is also true in the negative!

Mark Twain famously said, *"I am an old man and have known a great many troubles, most of which never happened! Worrying is like paying a debt that you don't owe! I have spent most of my life worrying about things that never happened!"*

If you are constantly thinking of negative things—whether they are true or not—your outlook on life can't help but be negative.

If however you can focus on the positive—finding the positive in a negative world—your outlook will be positive.

Consider Paul and Silas; they had been mistreated, beaten badly and cast into the deepest prison in the city of Philippi. What was their reaction? They were singing and praising God at midnight! No wonder God opened the doors and set them free!

They had a firm grasp of their reality. They were not pretending that they were free and that they had not been beaten. **BUT they looked beyond the prison** to where Jesus is sitting at the right hand of God the Father and that caused them to rejoice! When they considered the greatness of God's mercy it caused them to sing out loud until all of the other prisoners heard them!

Their story is told in Acts 16:16-40.

They could have bemoaned their sad plight and they would have been factually correct—**BUT they chose to think about Jesus and His grace and mercy!**

It doesn't take great intellect to find the negative in life—just read the paper or watch the news! You don't have to have either integrity or morality to be a pessimist. But to rise up after being knocked down takes a peculiar strength that not too many possess.

That special something is a belief! It takes faith that you belong up and not down!

If you believe that God has a good future for you regardless of your present circumstances or situations you are not deluded—you are walking in faith in the unseen.

The unseen world is more real than the one you can see and touch. It is the eternal place, while this world is only a temporary abode.

Our cry to God should be the same as that godly man Job. He realized that there was more that he did not know than what he could imagine.

He cried out to God, *"Teach me what I do not see"* Job 34:32.

And consider how much Job suffered! Yet his latter end was greater than his former. The key to Job's recovery lay in his ability to trust God. Putting your faith in the unseen opens the door for God to put vision within your heart.

Would it surprise you to find out that God has an imagination?

The imagination of God is limitless.

He imagined everything in His heart before He created any of it.

He saw the robin fly before there was even a planet for it to fly on.

He watched the grasshopper chew on a blade of grass before either existed.

He knew beforehand exactly what a porpoise, seal, whale and a shark would be like before He even created the water for them to swim in.

As you look at this amazing world we live in it is evident that our God loves colors and flowers and sunsets and beautiful mountain ranges.

He also loves ants, bees and spiders.

He created it all and more in His mind before He spoke it out of His mouth.

To be like God means a lot of things to a lot of people. We all agree that God is love, He is pure and holy. But He also possesses an extraordinary intellect and imagination.

God isn't just the Creator, *He is creative*. He hasn't changed.

It makes me sad when I consider that Christians, who ought to be more God-like than other people, lack imagination.

If there is anything that annoys me it is when God's people refuse to imagine anything even slightly new or different in their lives. And they demand that nothing ever changes in their day to day living and especially in their church. *"Exactly as it used to be is how I want it to stay!"* seems to be the motto of so many.

They claim to have daily discussions with the God of the Universe, the Supreme architect of life, He who instantly invented billions of galaxies and named each star within those galaxies!

He who created such a vast amount of life on this planet that we are still discovering new life every year is not stuck in a rut! He was the Creator and He still is!

If there is a reason why our church services sometimes are boring I believe some of the reason is simply that we lack imagination. We **EXPECT** the same thing every week. We **EXPECT** nothing to change.

That is why churches split over the color of carpet!

That is why music has become divisive. Good Lord!

Do we not realize that everything on this dirty little planet wears out?

New churches will one day be torn down!

Modern music will one day be out of style.

Haircuts change, styles change, favorite colors and favorite foods change.

The Christian who refuses to imagine new things is bound to be stuck in the past.

God makes all things new!

"Remember not the former things, nor consider the things of old. Behold, I am doing a new thing; now it springs forth, do you not perceive it?" Isaiah 43:18-19.

He wants us to have God sized visions, to dream God sized dreams!

"In the last days it shall be, God declares, that I will pour out my Spirit on all flesh, and your sons and your daughters shall prophesy, and your young men shall see visions, and your old men shall dream dreams" Acts 2:17

All Christians should be forward thinking in their outlook. The early church certainly was. What happened to the body of Christ to where now it either can't think of the future or it just won't?

I recently spent time with a genuine 60's hippy. He still dressed in bell-bottom pants, tie-died shirt and had long hair and a beard. He sat around listening to Cream and other 60's bands. He even said, *"It's a conspiracy man!"* I couldn't help but laugh inside! **He was stuck!**

He didn't work. He refused to adapt. He held on to the past because it was where he actually lived.

I walked away thinking to myself how much he had in common with many modern Christians!

They fell into a rut and liked it! They comfortably fit into it and decided that it was safe and secure. Soon they stopped looking outside of their personal rut and stopped being or doing anything for God.

A rut is nothing but a long grave!

Anyone who falls into and stays in a rut is as dead spiritually as if he already had a tombstone placed over his head.

Is your God dull? If He is then you don't know Him very well.

We place artificial limits on God to make Him more appealing to our tastes.

That is why there is a debate over the new and old songs.

Do we think that God has a small hymnal in heaven?

Where did we get the idea that God only likes Southern Gospel? Or only contemporary? Or classical?

How is it even possible that the God who created such an infinite amount and variety of life on this planet only likes a couple certain types of music?

I am 100% certain that the music in heaven puts our very best efforts to shame.

If God has such an enormous imagination why don't we?

I once performed a funeral service for an elderly man in his 80's. I didn't know the family so I asked his widow and children what he was like. They stared off into space for a few minutes before answering me.

"He ate the same thing for breakfast every day of our 62 years of marriage" the wife said. *"Post Toasties."*

I was expecting a little more than that, so I pressed them on what he liked to do. *"Did he fish, travel or do anything interesting?"* I asked.

"No, he just worked, came home and kept to his routine" she said. Her children just nodded their heads in agreement.

When it came time for the service a grand total of 5 people showed up to celebrate the life of a man who inhabited this planet for over 80 years!

<u>5 people</u>; his wife and their two children and their spouses. That was all!

He had no neighbors although he lived in that neighborhood for over 40 years.

No coworkers although he had worked his entire adult life at one factory alongside of hundreds of other people.

No friends, no associates—nobody. His impact on this planet was negligible. One might say he never lived at all.

What would you say his vision was of himself?

Apparently he had no vision besides breathing. If that is a depiction of your life then I counsel you to pick up your bible and start putting God's Word into your soul.

It is a mystery how anyone can read the thousands of promises contained in the bible and not get excited about their future.

God has promised forgiveness. 1 John 1:9 says, *"If we confess our sins, He is faithful and just to forgive us our sins and to cleanse us from all unrighteousness."*

God promises our sins will be far removed from us. Psalm 103:12 says, *"As far as the east is from the west, so far has He removed our transgressions from us."*

We are promised that our sins will be buried. Micah 7:19 says, *"He will again have compassion on us, and will subdue our iniquities. You will cast all our sins into the depths of the sea."*

We are promised the Holy Spirit. In Luke 11:13 Jesus said, *"If you then, being evil, know how to give good gifts to your children, how much more will your heavenly Father give the Holy Spirit to those who ask Him!"*

The Lord Jesus promised that the Holy Spirit will guide you and show you the truth. John 16:13, *"when He, the Spirit of truth, is come, He will guide you into all truth: for He shall not speak of himself; but whatsoever He shall hear, that shall He speak: and He will shew you things to come."*

God gave the best He had by giving us His only Son. Romans 8:32 says, *"He who did not spare His own Son, but delivered Him up for us all, how shall He not with Him also freely give us all things?"*

I could go on and on!

There are thousands of promises contained in God's Word.

We just have to believe the Word for ourselves.

We must become convinced of this one truth; either God's Word is wholly true to me or it is wholly false. It can't be both.

Will you believe God or not?

If you will believe His Word it is like you have opened a door for God to come in to your heart and life. Then He can start working on you to change you.

But understand this; He will never work at odds with His Word the bible. So putting your faith in His Word is essential.

Do you believe that *"I can do all things through Christ who strengthens me!"*? Philippians 4:13. Either you can do all things or else the scripture is a lie! Which is it?

Before you make excuses why you can't do something perhaps you should consider the evidence to the contrary.

A little 7 year old boy in Texas was convinced of the need for a border wall. He went to work trying to raise money to fund the wall. He sold hot chocolate for $2 per cup. How did he do? Well, he has raised over $22 thousand dollars at the time of this writing.

Now suppose some saint had decided to do something like that for missions?

The real question is, "*Why didn't some saint do that first?*"

There are millions of examples of people who used their God-given imaginations to achieve something for God and His kingdom.

There was a little home-bound widow woman who could no longer go to church due to her failing health. She had never missed church in her life and she became terribly depressed for a while when she couldn't go.

But thankfully she actually knew God personally, <u>so some of His personality rubbed off on her.</u>

Picking up her local phone book she began to work her way through it, starting with the A's.

Going down each page she would call the number and tell them who she was and that she was only calling to pray with them if they would permit it.

Amazingly in only one year that little widow led over 200 people to a saving knowledge of Jesus Christ! All from her home over the phone!

If you cannot see it then you will never achieve it.

Vision is simply another name for imagination.

If you have been wounded deeply it is easy to **ONLY SEE** yourself as wounded.

If God sees you as healed, worthy, lovely, and redeemed who is right, you or God?

Your imagination is small and weak if all you see is failure.

What is your definition of failure anyway?

In 1912 a missionary named Dr. William Leslie went to live and minister to tribal people in a remote corner of the Congo. After 17 years he returned to the U.S. a broken and discouraged man. He believed that he had failed to even make an impact in the Congo.

But in 2010, a team of missionaries made a surprising discovery. There was a whole group of churches that had sprung up from the work of Dr. Leslie! Those churches were not just surviving, they were thriving and reproducing.

He saw very little results in his lifetime in the natural and died wondering if he had missed God somehow. We know that he was in the perfect will of God and he was anything but a failure—**_NOW!_** But he never realized what an impact he had on those precious people.

You don't have to be great among men to be famous in heaven!

Start imagining yourself to be the way that God sees you and the way that He imagines you to be!

You are a king and a priest unto God! That means you have authority over God's enemies and access to God's presence anytime you want it.

You are a child of God! That means that your family, which happens to rule the universe, is on your side always and forever!

You are loved supremely by God! He gladly sent His own precious Son Jesus Christ to die in your place so that He could have you as His child. That is love that has no limits!

You are precious to Him!

He thinks of you constantly!

His plans for you are fantastic!

He has a chair picked out for you to sit in at His table!

He has a new name picked out for you that only He knows!

He longs to hold you in His arms and to show you His love!

He has chosen a robe that will fit you just perfectly!

Wow! You have an amazing future with God!

That ought to perk up even the sourest old grouch!

However if you are stuck in a rut, whether it is of your own creation or someone forced you into it, you must begin immediately to imagine life outside of that rut.

Unless you can see a new life you will probably never experience it.

Have you ever considered the Wright Brothers and the first sustained flight?

Can you imagine what it felt like for Orville to lift off in his powered plane? Think of it, he was running headlong into a 27 mph wind which gave him lift and he became the first man to fly a powered aircraft.

Do you know how long that first flight lasted? _It lasted all of 12 seconds and reached an incredible speed of 6.8 mph!_

That sounds pretty small now, but it was the result of literally thousands of hours of research and hard work to get that 12 seconds.

You know what else it took a great deal of? It took a lot of shared imagination on their part!

We use imagination every day in thousands of different ways. We cook and clean and wash and dry things by imagination. We think of what the finished product will be. Ultimately, imagination influences everything we do regardless of our profession.

What you imagine is your map. However you design it to be is the direction that you will take.

If you think that God can't forgive you then your effort will usually be centered on trying to win God's approval.

You will have fallen into the trap that tells us that if we really work at it hard God will forgive us. That is a lie from the devil!

<u>You can't EARN forgiveness because Jesus has already **PAID FOR IT!**</u>

You were bought with a great price because God loved you BEFORE you were a Christian. If He loved you that much while you were a sinner how much more do you think that He loves you now?

"This is love, not that we have loved God but that he loved us and sent his Son to be the propitiation for our sins." <u>1 John 4:10.</u>

In your relationship with God you must have an imagination that is based on what God believes! It is not about imagining yourself being rich and famous! **It is about being what God imagines you to be.**

It isn't based only on what you think or imagine! It is solely based on what God thinks and imagines for you.

God has a powerful imagination!

Consider this promise that was given to the tribe of Judah after the Babylonians had conquered them;

"For I know the plans I have for you, declares the LORD, plans for welfare and not for evil, to give you a future and a hope. Then you will call upon me and come and pray to me, and I will hear you. You will seek me and find me, when you seek me with all your heart. I will be found by you, declares the LORD, and I will restore your fortunes!" <u>Jeremiah 29:11-14</u>

At the time that God spoke this word Judah was crushed, defeated and without hope! But God imagined a day where they would be restored, happy and blessed!

It is imagination until it becomes a reality. God could see it in His heart and mind.

When you pray how do you envision the Lord? Is He paying attention to you? Do you feel that you have to remind Him who you are? Or do you spend most of your prayer time apologizing to God for some past failure?

Beloved if that is how you approach God you haven't been reading the right scriptures!

Go back and read the promises found in Jeremiah 29:11-15 again and rehearse to yourself what God wants to do in your life.

How do you see Jesus when you pray to Him?

Is he attentive?

Is he disinterested in what you have to say?

Or do you see Jesus lean forward on His throne to eagerly look into your face?

Is your conception of Christ one of Him smiling at you because He is glad to hear your voice?

Your heart image of Christ is Who you are praying to! So make that image biblically correct!

If you believe in your heart that Christ is not interested in you and that He barely knows your name you are not likely to pray with much faith.

If you see yourself as unloved your mental image is faulty, your faith is weak and your knowledge is defective!

When you pray see Jesus as John saw Him!

Then I turned to see the voice that was speaking to me, and on turning I saw seven golden lampstands, and in the midst of the lampstands one like a son of man, clothed with a long robe and with a golden sash around his chest. The hairs of his head were white, like white wool, like snow. His eyes were like a flame of fire, his feet were like burnished bronze, refined in a furnace, and his voice was like the roar of many waters. In his right hand he held seven stars, from his mouth came a sharp two-edged sword, and his face was like the sun shining in full strength. When I saw him, I fell at his feet as though dead. Revelation 1:12-17

When you are praying **THAT IS WHO YOU ARE TALKING TO!!!**

That is how He looks!!

Picture Him in your mind that way and you will also want to fall at His feet!

He is mighty, powerful and awesome, but He is also gentle, easy to be entreated and He is love personified.

If your mental roadmap is blank it is because you have no imagination. You have almost no expectations. You haven't filled in the map with anything beautiful.

You are stuck in your past, in your hurts or in your fears.

All you see is all you have.

That takes very little faith and almost no talent.

Believing in what God says will change your outlook on life and will give you hope for your future.

Have you ever travelled to a new place?

Can you remember what it was like to see new things?

Did you imagine what it would be like?

For years I longed to see real mountains. I had seen pictures and had seen the scenery in movies, but I had never seen them for myself.

So when I finally got to Colorado and saw them up close it was awe inspiring!

I had imagined them but in reality they were more grand and beautiful than I had imagined.

It was my imagination that caused me to drive across Missouri, Kansas and Colorado to see them. I visualized them until it had become a longing in my heart to go.

Your imagination can be a help or a hindrance; the choice is up to you.

If you imagine that when you go into a bank to get a loan everyone will be glad to see you it will show on your face that you are more positive.

Those positivity cues are read instinctively by those whose livelihood is dealing with people.

A man who slinks into the bank looking all down in the mouth and depressed is not an attractive loan candidate. Even if the bank manager doesn't think in those exact words he will feel it.

If however that same man dressed nice and visualized himself as a child of the King of the universe he will project a positive and friendly demeanor.

That doesn't mean that he will get the loan, but at least he will be able to speak with the loan officer. Some people lose before they walk through the door—all because they imagine themselves to be losers.

You can imagine almost anything that your physical senses can detect; smells, sounds, and feelings can be imagined.

You need to unleash the God-given power of your imagination for your own good.

Everyone who ever achieved great things started out to achieve SOMETHING. It might not have gone according to plan but they were definitely struggling to achieve something.

A person who tries to achieve nothing usually succeeds. A person who attempts to achieve something always succeeds, even if he ends up doing something different than what he set out to do.

That is why it is so important for the Christian to study God's Word and to meditate on its promises.

Get those promises into your heart and mind and you will start thinking positively!

Start seeing what God sees and you will start believing what God believes!

"Thus says the LORD who made the earth, the LORD who formed it and established it, the LORD is His name: Call to me and I will answer you, and will tell you great and hidden things that you have not known." Jeremiah 33:2-3.

God is saying to us that ***if we will allow Him to***, He will increase our vision! He will help us to see greater things than we thought possible. Nothing shall be impossible to you!

*"For truly, I say to you, if you have faith like a grain of mustard seed, you will say to this mountain, 'Move from here to there,' and it will move, **and nothing will be impossible for you**."* Matthew 17:20.

God doesn't see you as a failure! He truly sees what He can do in your life as a reality. He has faith is in His abilities to transform your brokenness until you are 100% whole. He believes that He can do anything, even through you! Do you believe that He can?

God has used a whale, worm, donkey, dove, ravens, plants, wind, rain, and even a rooster to achieve His will—he can use you too!

Child of God stop seeing yourself as a failure!

Stop seeing only your hurts.

Start seeing what God sees in you!

If you are defined by your hurts, failures and defeats then how exactly are you like God?

Jesus suffered terribly, **but it never defined Him.**

Jesus seemed to be defeated on the cross; naked He hung there, bloody and battered, mocked and ridiculed by the masses. **But that never defined Him.**

<u>Jesus knew that God thought differently of Him than people did.</u>

He knew that even His own mother and brothers didn't believe in Him, *but He knew that His Father did!*

He knew that His disciples—His closest friends—didn't understand Him at all! *Yet He knew what His Father thought and that was more than enough!*

Are you really any different than Him?

People try to define you by status, gender, failure, or success, fame or shame, **but ultimately their opinions don't matter if God thinks differently.**

Go with what your Father says and thinks!

IF GOD SAYS YOU ARE A SUCCESS then you are not a failure, even if the whole world says that you are!

How you see yourself through the eyes of others will bring you down, and it is not even based on reality.

If you see yourself the way that God sees you then you will believe that God can take a lump of coal and make a diamond out of it.

God prefers using base things, broken things, useless things and things that the world casts off to do extraordinary things with.

Instead of imagining yourself defeated, try imagining yourself the way that God sees you!

You are a King—a Priest—a child of the King! You are mighty in Christ!

So instead of focusing on what your body or your enemies might say about you, try focusing on what God is going to do in your life!

It took a while for me to realize this, but most of the problems I have dealt with in my life were self-inflicted.

It seemed to be that misery and tragedy were out of my control. I always felt like a victim! Those things were actually magnified by the negative mindset that I had.

Every attack, setback or failure only intensified my belief that I was cursed and nothing would ever change.

I chose to think negatively and poorly about my life. While I didn't have the power to control my circumstances, I surely had the power to control my mindset, but I didn't want to. **Being negative actually gave me an excuse for failing in life!**

But then I met Jesus! I found that He makes all things new—including me, my mind and my attitude!

You are powerful in Jesus!

"Therefore I will boast all the more gladly of my weaknesses, so that the power of Christ may rest upon me. For when I am weak, then I am strong." 2 Corinthians 12:9-10

"I can do all things through Christ who strengthens me." Philippians 4:13

READ IT IN THE WORD, SEE IT AND BELIEVE IT!

Chapter 7: Bringing healing to the Body

> *"Tomorrow and the plans for tomorrow can have no significance at all unless you are in full contact with the reality of the present, since it is only in the present that you live!"* **Alan Watts.**

It is difficult sometimes to get healing after suffering a tragedy. The reality of the pain and wounding is too real to simply pretend that it doesn't exist.

I often counsel people who have suffered a great trauma such as the loss of a loved one that they will grieve, so it is better to allow themselves to do it. Holding it in only forces your soul to grieve in other ways.

One person came to me and asked for prayer. It seems that for the past year or so they were having sudden outbursts of anger. They had never had that problem before and didn't know where it came from.

Being familiar with them I was able to deduce that it actually started when they lost their mother. They had a really hard time coming to terms with her sudden and unexpected death and never really got closure. Her outbursts were symptoms of grief. The answer to her problem was to get closure.

The reason why I bring this up is because many people cannot process their trauma and they are basically in a grieving place without understanding how to get out.

We cannot stay in that place of torment and grief. That is not to say that we will not grieve—for we will. But if we can't get closure on the *"why's"* of someone dying, or *"why"* someone hurt us, at least we can rest in the knowledge that the Lord loves us and He will take care of our unanswered *"why's."*

We have to give our grief to Him. We have to cast all of our hurts, cares and worries upon Him.

One lady lost her newborn baby daughter. Her heart was so broken that she simply felt as if she couldn't go on any more. She even prayed that the Lord would take her life.

One day the hospital where her little baby died called her.

A nurse was on the line and she asked if it would be possible for the lady to come see her in the maternity ward.

At first the woman didn't want to go because that is where her baby died, but eventually she relented and went.

When she got there the kind nurse took her to see a poor little baby girl. It was born premature and addicted to meth. Its mother had abandoned it with the hospital.

The nurse explained that the little girl needed constant love and attention.

It lay there crying and shaking and the lady began to cry. Here was a baby that needed a mother and didn't have one. She was a mother who didn't have a baby.

Picking up the little baby caused it to shake and scream even more. The drugs that the mother had taken had gotten into its system and now it was having withdrawals.

It was also frightened. That baby needed to be held from the moment of delivery but had not been.

Holding the little bundle tightly the mother imagined that it was her little girl. How would she feel if that were her baby? She would love it and care for it and speak soothing words over it. So she decided that if that baby's mother wouldn't love her, she would.

For the next few weeks she came to the hospital every day just to hold the baby. Soon the little girl stopped shivering and crying when she picked her up. Soon she was relaxing when she heard the woman's voice. It was obvious that they had bonded.

So a social worker helped her to adopt her baby girl.

This is a true story and I want you to notice a couple of things about it.

First, loving another baby never erased the hurt of losing her own.

Secondly, she was capable of loving another even though losing hers was so devastating.

She was faced with a choice, just as all who have suffered are; **will I stay in this place of hurting or will I venture out into the sunlight again?**

It is not easy. It may not be quick. But it is very possible that God can give you your joy back.

He can cause you to learn to love again, to trust again and to reach out to others in grace.

Only those who have been terribly wounded understand how other survivors feel.

I sat down with a couple some years ago who had asked to talk with me. This is fairly normal and I didn't expect too much to happen—***boy was I wrong!***

They came with an agenda!

We expect Christians to give grace to others, and it is a shock to our system when they don't.

There were a few people in our church that they wanted to see run out! I couldn't believe my ears.

They were not suggesting either! They were telling me who they were and what I was going to do.

I let them vent for a while and then I said to them as quietly and softly as I could, *"So how come you want justice for others and not for yourselves?"*

Yikes! They exploded at me!

Those two were not perfect saints—far from it.

Their lives were not perfect, their walk with God was far from perfect, they fought constantly, and when they weren't fighting they were bickering. They had many issues of their own.

Yet they were not there to ask for help with their lives; **they were there to destroy other people's lives.**

Can you imagine what a church would be like that just ran people out because someone was jealous, or hated their haircut, or seemed too confident for their liking?

We wouldn't have anybody left!

Amazingly I was able to dig through the garbage and trash that they were spewing and find out the real cause of their rage—***she had caught him cheating.***

And instead of dealing with their issues they were trying to fix other people!

All of her anger issues—**and she had plenty!**—were rooted in her failing marriage.

She was hurting, but she was dealing with it all wrong. Instead of getting help she was doing what hurting people tend to do and that is hurt other people.

Once I got down to what was really driving them it was as if the curtain was pulled back and the truth was obvious. This didn't make them like me! It had the opposite effect and they quickly left the church.

Last time I saw them (*many years later*) they were still bitter and still fought constantly.

It is an important lesson for us to consider **that just because someone is hurting you does not mean that they aren't hurting too.**

But James said *"For he shall have judgment without mercy, that hath showed no mercy!"* James 2:13.

So we must show mercy! We have no choice!!!

DO NOT BECOME WHAT HAS HURT YOU!

Don't break someone's heart just because yours has been broken.

Don't become cruel because someone was cruel to you.

Don't hurt someone just because you have been hurt.

Don't become emotionless because you weren't shown the emotion you deserve.

And don't become the person who hurt you.

<u>We always have two options in life when things don't go how we want them to go;</u>

We can move on with a positive attitude believing that God will take care of us and our situation

Or we can hang our heads and sulk over what could have been and live in our self-imposed misery.

If we give our lives to Jesus we can be sure that He will set about putting our lives back together again—He is a master carpenter after all!

Trusting—***fully trusting*** in the Savior means giving Him everything you have! Hurts, failures, desires, dreams and anything else that defines you must be given to Him without hesitation!

We can only surrender everything to Him if we understand that He alone is able to sympathize with us in our weaknesses and hurts! He alone knows what we are going through! Nobody else can understand like Jesus can!

Abandoned;

Have you ever felt alone? I mean completely abandoned and without hope? Jesus felt that in a measure that we cannot fathom. He had always been united with the Father. He had always listened and heard the Father's voice in His heart. He had never known any type of separation from God!

When He was baptized at the Jordan River the Spirit of God who had been with Him took up residence in Him. From that time on according to the bible Jesus operated completely under the control of the Holy Spirit—God's Spirit. See Acts 10:38.

That level of unity is actually difficult for us to comprehend.

From childhood Jesus knew to choose the good and hate the evil.

"Therefore the Lord himself shall give you a sign; Behold, a virgin shall conceive, and bear a son, and shall call his name Immanuel. Butter and honey shall he eat, that he may know to refuse the evil, and choose the good." Isaiah 7:14-15

"And the spirit of the LORD shall rest upon him, the spirit of wisdom and understanding, the spirit of counsel and might, the spirit of knowledge and of the fear of the LORD; And shall make him of quick understanding in the fear of the LORD: and he shall not judge after the sight of his eyes, neither reprove after the hearing of his ears." Isaiah 11:2-3

Jesus was practiced in obeying the Spirit's guidance His whole life. He was born with the same nature as we are, yet He refused to obey His fleshly nature and instead obeyed God His Father.

Total obedience was what He knew and all that He knew.

If you think about it, we know more about separation from God than we do about unity with God. We were born sinful. We have a sin-nature, and we yield to it every time that we get angry and act out, or take what isn't ours.

The average child has to be taught to be good because it isn't in his default programming! His program tells him to take his brother's cookie or toy if he wants it and to throw a temper-tantrum if he doesn't get what he wants when he wants it!

But Jesus refused to yield to the sin-nature and He never sinned! **NEVER!**

"For our sake he made him to be sin who knew no sin." 2 Corinthians 5:21.

"You were ransomed from the futile ways inherited from your forefathers, not with perishable things such as silver or gold, but with the precious blood of Christ, like that of a lamb without blemish or spot." 1 Peter 1:28-29

"How much more will the blood of Christ, who through the eternal Spirit offered himself without blemish to God, purify our conscience from dead works to serve the living God." Hebrews 9:14

Jesus was the spotless and sinless Lamb of God! He had never known a time in His life where God wasn't with Him.

But then He was crucified!

For six long hours Jesus hung on that cruel cross suffering unimaginable pain for man's sins. Slowly His precious blood trickled down the cross and dripped on that hard ground.

That was the terrible cost of our salvation, and it was exceedingly high!

For the first three hours as Jesus bore the punishment God was with Him.

This is probably not something that most people consider *but God partook of the suffering with His Son*!

It wasn't until the last three hours that God's Spirit pulled away from Christ. For the first three hours of agony the Spirit of God gave Jesus the comfort of His presence.

You must ask yourself why God chose to stay with the One that He had consigned to bear our sins.

I believe that the answer why God the Father chose to stay with His Son even though our sins were placed on Him is found in us!

How many times has God's Spirit strove with us as we yield to temptations and sin? Haven't we felt His Holy Spirit being grieved by our actions? Why didn't He just pull away from us immediately when we sinned against Him?

The answer why He doesn't abandon us even though we commit a sin is that He loves us.

Don't misunderstand me; God will eventually leave you if you persist in sinful living.

But I am speaking of some sins that trip us as we are trying to walk the Christian life. Maybe you get mad and speak out when the Spirit is trying to get you to hold your peace. Perhaps you lust when He is convicting you for looking at something bad.

Whatever it may be there are times when we fail God. But He stays for as long as possible because He loves us!

Beloved I am confident in this; all of us occasionally grieve God's Spirit! We do things that cause Him pain and discomfort. In our lives we usually separate ourselves from pain or from people who make us feel uncomfortable, but the Spirit stays with us! *It takes a lot to make Him leave!*

But even with Christ there came a point when the Spirit of God could no longer abide in Him. As the sun rose to mark noon it suddenly withdrew its shining and the land became dark as night. It was no eclipse of the moon; it was rather an eclipse of the heart of God and Christ!

Darkness came between Him and His Son! The sins of the world were placed upon His sinless form and He who knew no sin became sin for you and me.

As Jesus hung upon the cross and the sun withdrew it's shining the people realized something amazing was happening, but they did not know what it was or why it was happening. If they had only known how important this time of complete separation was for their eternal destinies they would have rejoiced to see it!

For three solid hours the Savior of mankind was completely, totally abandoned by the Father and the Spirit! He was alone. For the first and only time in His existence, Jesus the Son of God was totally alone!

Don't miss this important point! Jesus had never known what it was like to be separated from the Father!

That was one of the things that He kept repeating to the Jews;

"And he who sent me is with me. He has not left me alone, for I always do the things that are pleasing to him." John 8:29

"Yet I am not alone, for the Father is with me." John 16:32

But at noon on crucifixion Friday Jesus the Son of God felt God His Father pull His Holy Spirit from Him!

That had to have been the most awful feeling ever!

In God's presence there is peace, power, assurance, joy, love and everything else that God is!

But when His presence is gone those things are also gone, and the opposite takes their place.

Instead of peace you will have dread and fear.

Instead of power you will feel overwhelmingly weak and frail.

Instead of assurance you will feel doubt. Instead of joy you will have sorrow.

Instead of love you will feel that you are hated!

The lack of God's presence to someone who has never KNOWN it is horrible. But to One who ONLY KNEW what it was like to have the constant presence of God to lose it was nothing short of terror. Only hell itself could be worse.

Without the presence of the Spirit Jesus had to have faith in God the Father!

Without the Holy Spirit's presence guiding the Lord Jesus He had to only believe the Word of God. He could not feel the Father's presence nor the Spirit's guidance. He felt no peace! He felt only sorrow and rejection!

For three hours the Lord Jesus operated on FAITH ALONE.

He did not go on His feelings, for they told Him that He was forsaken and unloved. He absolutely could not trust what He felt!

Faith is not feeling!

Faith is the trust that what God has said is true no matter the circumstances!

This is what each of us must understand; Jesus put His faith in the written promises of the Old Testament. Those promises told Him that He would die and be resurrected on the third day.

Nowhere does the bible tell us that the Holy Spirit was with Christ the last three hours of His life!

He stood on faith in God's Word in spite of what He saw, felt or heard!

That is what we must do too!

We must trust the Lord Jesus because He knows separation and suffering on a scale that is way beyond anything anyone else could ever know. He alone can understand what you are going through.

We are going to have to trust the Father that He loves us even in the darkest times just as the Lord Jesus trusted the Father when He could no longer feel His presence.

In spite of what we feel, hear, see or think we must trust God's Word!

In spite of what people may say about us or to us we must trust God's Word!

In spite of circumstances, loneliness or heartache we must trust God's Word!

"Who shall separate us from the love of Christ? Shall tribulation, or distress, or persecution, or famine, or nakedness, or danger, or sword? For I am sure that neither death nor life, nor angels nor rulers, nor things present nor things to come, nor powers, nor height nor depth, nor anything else in all creation, will be able to separate us from the love of God in Christ Jesus our Lord." Romans 8:35, 38-39

You must trust His Word because He knows what all of the temptations and trials and sorrows and heartaches are like! He knows!

If we are ever going to be the people that God wants us to be we are going to have to stop waiting on feelings and start trusting God's Word!

Too many people never believe God for their own deliverance and yet they are trying to set others free.

If you have major issues you should get them reconciled with the Savior before you attempt to conquer the world brother or sister!

Nobody wants us trying to bandage them if we're bleeding all over the place.

One minister spoke to me about something that was troubling him. He related how that he wanted to "*get back into preaching*" but that every time he tried to it seemed his past kept coming back to him. All of those failures and hurts kept flooding his heart and mind until he wanted to quit the ministry all over again.

God spoke to me that I was to tell him this, "You have never let God heal you yet, and so you are not ready to help anyone else. If you are bleeding on them you will not do them any good. Get alone with God and let Him show you why He keeps bringing up your past."

Beloved we must be healed!

I fear that spiritually speaking we have a large segment of our churches that are walking wounded. They are not prepared to fight the devil because they are still bleeding spiritually speaking.

If our lives are an unmitigated disaster we ought to go to God and let Him fix us so that we can help others. But until we can be honest with God and surrender our whole lives to Him we are not going to get set free.

If you have ever flown on a large airplane you have seen them give the preflight safety instructions.

The one that I always pay attention to is the one where the stewardess explains what to do if the air masks drop down.

They always make it a point to tell you to put the mask on yourself before you attempt to help anyone else.

The reason why they do this is because unless you are getting air in your lungs you will become a liability instead of an asset.

The spiritual application also applies; unless we get healed we will become a liability also.

Every attempt that we make to help others will result in our bleeding on them. We will infect every situation with our sickness.

I counsel you beloved, go to Jesus and spend time in His presence. Get filled with the Holy Spirit and allow Him to delve deep into your heart and soul until He can pull out the junk, hurts, wickedness and anything else that is lurking there.

Only when He has complete control of us will we be worthy vessels that He can use.

"A large house contains not only vessels of gold and silver, but also of wood and clay. Some indeed are for honorable use, but others are for common use. **So if anyone cleanses himself of what is unfit, he will be a vessel for honor:** *sanctified, useful to the Master, and prepared for every good work."* 2 Timothy 2:20-21.

You want to be a vessel of honor! And the only way to become one is to yield to God everything you are and have.

That is what the Lord Jesus did, and it is what we all must do.

Do you remember in chapter one of this book how I explained to you that the Jews will be amazed to find marks of the crucifixion on their Messiah?

"And they shall ask him, What are these wounds in thine hands? Then he shall answer, 'Those with which I was wounded in the house of my friends.'" Zechariah 13:6.

Did you notice the almost nonchalant way that the bible describes how Jesus explained his wounds to the Jews? *"Those with which I was wounded in the house of my friends"* He answered them.

He didn't take the opportunity to explain how wrongly and unjustly His people had treated Him.

He wasn't parading His hurts so that everyone would know what happened to Him.

No, Jesus was busy saving them and they were the ones who noticed that He had wounds consistent with a crucifixion.

We can learn much from the Lord's example.

He fully trusted in God while He hung alone on the cross.

He does not carry old hurts and insults around with Him!

He has fully given them to the Lord God His Father and that is where He has left them!

They do not define His reality! They are part of His experience, and He is not ashamed of those wounds! But He doesn't feel the need to show everyone His hurts!

So why do we think we need to show everyone each of our bruises, cuts, wounds and hurts?

Do we really need their approval so much that we shamefully exhibit each insult for them to see?

What is it that is lacking in us that we let our hurts define us so much?

Why must people keep their wounds open? Why must they keep them fresh and not let them heal?

If we are always proving our martyrdom to people it is proof that we are not yet healed and we are not yet ready to help anyone.

Living in God's light means that He shows us the hidden things that are lurking in the shadows—even when those shadows and hidden things are in our own hearts.

You must choose to walk in the Spirit!

You must choose to rejoice in the Lord!

You must choose to bless instead of cursing!

You must choose to pray for those who despitefully use you and harm you!

Remember that we are commanded to bless those who despitefully use us.

Show mercy, even when they are doing their dead-level best to destroy you and you will be shown much mercy from God.

I mentioned in the beginning of this book the word ***"skandal."***

It is mentioned 17 times in the New Testament.

Other than Jesus, Paul is the main person who uses it.

In <u>Romans 14</u> Paul spends a great deal of time teaching Christians about scandalizing others.

"Therefore let us not pass judgment on one another any longer, but rather decide never to put a stumbling block or hindrance in the way of a brother." <u>Romans 14:13.</u>

It is not our place to pass judgment on anyone else. And to be honest you wouldn't really want the job if you had it.

I know there are some who would be easy to condemn, but of course I don't know their secrets or their true history.

Jesus knows everything about them. He may have witnessed many times when they were beaten by their mom's boyfriend for no reason. The Lord has a record of the abuse they endured.

Perhaps they are a monster now, but they didn't start out that way.

We must learn that if someone stole something from us it is not as important as that person's soul. We are going to leave every toy, tool, and possession here when we die, so why get so hung up on them now?

If we fail to place a higher value on people than things we are not being Christ-like.

He gave up all of heaven for us!

He gave up the wealth of the earth for us!

He gave up the opportunity to rule as a king in Israel for us!

He surrendered His life so that He could die for us!

Possessions come and go! Souls are forever.

Paul further says, *"If your brother is grieved by what you eat, you are no longer walking in love. By what you eat, <u>do not destroy the one for whom Christ died</u>."* Romans 14:15

In other words, just because it doesn't bother you doesn't mean that it is alright for you to do it.

Here is the rule for the Christian to live by—<u>***if it hurts any other person I shouldn't do it!!!***</u>

This brings us to a subject that I have noticed is epidemic in our society today **and that is gossip.**

Twitter and Facebook are gossip sites.

If you post something good it will be either ignored or trashed by mean-spirited people.

They are like buzzards sitting on a tree limb watching the road for fresh road-kill!

As soon as they see a dead animal those buzzards jump on it and start picking it apart.

That buzzard mentality in people is a spirit!

Think about a buzzard; they prefer to eat rotten, smelly things. Their greatest pleasure is when some animal gets sick and dies! And if they are caught or cornered their only defense is to vomit on you! If you consider the things that a buzzard eats you can understand why you would not want buzzard puke on you! And buzzards prefer the company of other buzzards.

I believe there are many buzzards in church!

They prefer to consume rotten gossip. They seem to get a morbid pleasure when someone fails and loses out with God. The stuff that comes out of their mouths is not sweet! It is rotten, slanderous, putrid gossip. And they love to congregate with other stinking old buzzards!

It is the spirit of this age and it is antichrist.

Christians are to build up, not tear down. God has no patience with gossips.

In fact God had to kill a bunch of the children of Israel *because they wouldn't stop grumbling and gossiping!*

In Proverbs Solomon compares gossiping to a **maul,** a **sword** and a **sharp arrow**. Proverbs 25:18.

The maul was more or less used to cause blunt-force trauma to a foe. As you swung it you were just hoping to break some bones or cause a concussion. You were intent on hurting them!

A maul is used for close up fighting.

An example of a maul is a husband and wife arguing with each other and one of them brings up something hurtful from the past. It is intended to do harm!

Bitter and harsh words are never intended to build up! Their only use is to wound deeply and to do permanent damage.

Let's face it, some people are just bitter and mean. They know that what they are saying is going to hurt you badly, but they say it anyway.

Racist people are maul swingers. They use words like a cruel weapon to denigrate and belittle others.

They will tag you with a title and then you are forced to try to defend yourself against it.

When people insult you with a made-up title such as calling you toxically masculine or any other made up thing do not fall into the trap of trying to prove yourself to them.

You must be aware of the fact that the maul swinger is trying to mutilate you and incapacitate you. They are not seeking dialogue, they are seeking to destroy. Avoid getting down to their level!

When we gossip in a way that mutilates a person's character we may be doing them permanent harm. Every word out of the mouth of a Christian should be good for building up, not for tearing down.

A sword is also for close up fighting, but it is more discreet. It is sharp and makes clean cuts.

The sword in Solomon's day was more like a long knife than the medieval sword of Europe. Those swords were long and bulky.

The sword that Solomon spoke of was short and could be hidden.

In fact there are a few instances from scripture of people hiding them and pulling them out on an enemy.

That was the case for David's general Joab. He hid his sword from view so that he could get close to a man he was jealous of named Amasa. And when he was close enough he struck him down with that sword!

"And Joab said to Amasa, "Is it well with you, my brother?" And Joab took Amasa by the beard with his right hand to kiss him. But Amasa did not observe the sword that was in Joab's hand. So Joab struck him with it in the stomach and spilled his entrails to the ground without striking a second blow, and he died." <u>2 Samuel 20:9-10.</u>

The sword can be hidden until it is too late.

A person who uses gossip as a sword often make themselves appear to be your friend, but they have evil on their minds. Just as Joab intended to kill Amasa but still called him brother.

The person who smiles to your face but talks about you behind your back is a sword-swinger.

People use the sword when they attack you so personally that they attempt to render you helpless.

If they call you a liar, you are left having to defend yourself.

If a woman calls her husband a poor provider, or attacks his manhood he will feel the need to defend himself.

The sword attacks always make you try to defend yourself. That is their design.

"Hide me from the secret plots of the wicked, from the throng of evildoers, who whet their tongues like swords, who aim bitter words like arrows, shooting from ambush at

the blameless, shooting at him suddenly and without fear."
Psalm 64:2-4

If you spend your time **with people who are always belittling you** to where you feel that you have to stand up for yourself **do yourself a huge favor and leave!**

You don't need that in your life.

You must learn that you don't have to defend against every lie that is told. Leave them to God.

If you react every time that the enemy yells your name you will never do anything else. He will monopolize your time and energy.

Don't fall for his tricks.

So what if people hear a lie about you? For every one that you refute the devil has probably told a thousand that you haven't heard. Let it go. Let God deal with justifying you.

The devil's trick is to get the Christians to spend their time and energy trying to disprove what he called them.

That is why his crowd comes up with names that are so opposite to the truth—so you will have to defend yourself.

Consider the name *"homophobic."*

It literally means you are afraid of men. Of course they use it to denote a fear of homosexuals. Anyone who disagrees with their stated belief is therefore accused of being *"Homophobic."*

Or if you disagree with Islam you are called *"Islamophobic."*

In reality you are not driven by fear at all but by a belief that a behavior is wrong or an ideology is mistaken. But they cannot dialogue with you if they have already painted you with racist, misogynistic or other terms. They have cut off all dialogue, and that is their intention.

That is how the sword works! It cuts off any chance of reconciliation. It ends all dialogue.

The arrow is for shooting at people from hidden places.

The gossip that shoots arrows at you does it from a safe distance, and they are the hardest to deal with some times.

Often they will start the gossip but lie when cornered and pretend that they have no idea what you are talking about. Trying to trace the origins of gossip is a waste of your time.

If we could look eye to eye with our adversary it would be easier, but the arrow slinger hides behind others and fires at us.

The only weapon against arrows is the shield of faith.

When God told us to use it He wasn't being metaphorical, He meant it.

Your faith must be in what God's Word says about you and your life. Otherwise the arrows of the devil can enter into your heart.

When the devil spreads gossip through back channels and hides himself from view don't go digging through people to find the source. Instead pull up your shield and proclaim the Word of God over your life.

Do not avenge yourself beloved! Let God take care of the devil and his crowd.

"Their tongue is a deadly arrow; it speaks deceitfully; with his mouth each speaks peace to his neighbor, but in his heart he plans an ambush for him. Shall I not punish them for these things? Declares the LORD!" Jeremiah 9:8-9

Yes, He will punish them and what they have done to you will roll back on top of them.

WHAT YOU SOW IS WHAT YOU WILL REAP WITH INTEREST!!

"Do not be deceived: God is not mocked, for whatever one sows, that will he also reap. For the one who sows to his own flesh will from the flesh reap corruption, but the one who sows to the Spirit will from the Spirit reap eternal life." Galatians 6:7-8

So sow good things and you will eventually reap good things!

And if that evil person keeps sowing evil things they will reap in their flesh the evil that they have sown.

I cannot control my neighbor's garden! I can only control my own. We each have our own responsibilities that we are given. So let us focus on what we can do and leave the reaping to God.

In church there will always be weak people and strong people.

I am not referring to popularity or abilities.

I am referring to faith. Some are very weak in the faith and barely make it from day to day.

Others are not the least bit worried about anything; their faith is firmly in the Savior.

Some will argue over the meaning of John 11:32—*Jesus wept!*

Others will have a God-given grasp of the Word and can break it down to bite size chunks with ease.

When the weak brother is offended, he will usually lose hope quickly.

When the strong brother is offended he will overlook it and go on.

The more mature you are the more you will put up with other people's weaknesses.

"We who are strong have an obligation to bear with the failings of the weak, and not to please ourselves. Let each of us please his neighbor for his good, to build him up." Romans 15:1-2

In other words, have patience and grace with them!

You must have patience with others just as Jesus has had patience with you,

Many Sunday school teachers and pastors have become exasperated when a person who has gone to church for 50 years doesn't know the basics of Christianity. **Age doesn't always equal maturity!**

Maturity for a Christian is to be like Christ. We are to be servants to others!

Jesus put others before Himself and became a servant to the people He created. That is how Christians should behave also.

"*Do nothing from selfish ambition or conceit,* **but in humility count others more significant than yourselves.**"
<u>Philippians 2:3</u>

To achieve this will take the power of the Holy Spirit working in us every hour of every day.

To Jesus, people were the greatest treasure on this earth. When the devil tried to tempt Him with worldly treasures he didn't have a chance, for Jesus didn't desire those things. He desired to seek and to save people!!

He saw them as poor lost sheep in need of help!

He saw them differently than anyone else on earth saw them.

If we are ever going to be Christ-like we too will have to start seeing people differently.

If they are not valuable to us then we do not see them like God did.

God saw the world for what it was—sinful! Yet He loved it enough to send His precious Son to die for that sinful world!

<u>Owning our mistakes</u>

If we have harmed another person we don't have a choice but to try to make amends—we must apologize!

"First be reconciled to your brother." **Matthew 5:24**

However there is nothing more exasperating than when someone does you harm and issues a non-apology apology!

That is one where they say things like, *"If you were hurt by what I said I'm truly sorry."*

That is not a real apology. It's a non-apology apology.

Picture a person walking down the sidewalk next to the highway.

A car careens off of the road and plows right over them!

Stopping a block later the driver comes back to where that person lays all crumpled and crushed from the impact of their vehicle.

Leaning over their shattered body they say, *"If you were hurt by something I did I am sorry."*

IF!?

What do you mean by IF?

That is not taking ownership of your mistake.

It is refusing to admit your fault.

"If you were offended by what I said I am sorry" is not an admission of guilt! It is an attempt to push the offense off onto another.

It is saying that *"I am not the least bothered by what I did, but you must be, so I am sorry you are bothered."*

That is like telling God, *"I don't see any problem with my sins, but apparently you do so I am sorry you feel that way."*

Try that on Judgment Day and see where it gets you!

God demands honesty!

Be honest!

"I hurt you! I am so sorry that I hurt you!" is an apology.

Do you remember when David sinned with Bathsheba?

He hid it for about a year. He no doubt thought that he had gotten away with it, but God was watching and waiting for the right time to deal with David.

When God confronted David through the prophet Nathan David instantly repented and admitted his error, but that could not stop judgment from falling on him.

He prayed a powerful prayer of repentance that is recorded in **Psalm 51**.

See how he repented, *"**I know my transgressions, and my sin is ever before me**. Against you, you only, have I sinned and done what is evil in your sight, so that you may be justified in your words and blameless in your judgment."* Psalm 51:3-4

He said, *"I see what I have done and it is sin!"*

He never excused it. He didn't try to blame anyone else.

David might have been able to blame Bathsheba for bathing in the open area of her home, but he didn't.

According to David there was only one person who was liable for his sin and that was David.

A man who had done much harm to a pastor and others in a church was called to account for the things that he had said.

That man had lied, gossiped and slandered most everyone in the church.

When confronted with the evidence he put his hand on his chin as if he was really contemplating what they were saying. And then he looked them straight in the eyes and said, *"I can see how you might be offended by the way that sounds, but I meant no harm."*

WHAT?!

That is ridiculous! Of course he meant to harm people or he wouldn't have said those terrible things in the first place.

He refused to take ownership of his mistakes.

If we are going to be the Temple of God Almighty we must become a place where love abounds.

True love demands truth in our hearts.

We cannot harbor evil and wicked thoughts because they will eventually destroy us.

God's Word warns us of the danger of allowing even a root of bitterness to reside in our hearts;

"See to it that no one fails to obtain the grace of God; that no "root of bitterness" springs up and causes trouble, and by it many become defiled." <u>Hebrews 12:15.</u>

That root can cause us to fail to obtain the grace of God.

It simply is not worth it.

If you have hurt people, go and apologize for hurting them!

<u>Own your mistakes!</u> Make restitution if you can.

If they refuse to forgive you then leave it with them and God, but you must get your heart right with God.

Hiding the truth or hiding from the truth is no way to walk with God.

What I am saying is not intended to belittle where you might be. Instead I am trying to get you to see that no matter how bad things may be you do not have to stay in that place.

In chapter 6 I dealt with imagination. I tried to impress upon you that *no matter where you are God has something better in mind for you.*

If you are one of those people that have decided that you are not going to be blessed you must change your thinking and what you say. You must start speaking and thinking like God.

If you are in a self-imposed prison of regrets and sorrows you must admit that **YOU ARE YOUR OWN JAILER!**

You hold the keys to your prison!

No devil is strong enough to keep you from enjoying the presence of God! He can be found in the most inhospitable places on earth.

He can come to where you are and enlightened your world! He will drive the darkness out of your heart and mind! Let Him in and let Him be God in you!

One man heard me preach on this subject and went home and really thought about it for a few days.

I will never forget when he called me later.

He said, *"Pastor, this is _____ and I have been thinking about what you said the other day. Pastor, I realize that I have been doing everything that God's Word condemns. I have hurt people, slandered them and gossiped about them.* **What do I do now?"**

I told him that if possible he needed to honestly apologize to anyone that he had hurt.

He said, *"That would be over a thousand people!"*

Can you imagine the impact his negative attitude had had on the church?

Can you imagine the image that his friends and neighbors had of the church because of what he had said?

Needless to say he had a lot of work to do.

But we all have a long way to go. It is my prayer that this book will point you in the right direction and start you on the right path.

The answers are all found in having a close relationship with the Savior. Get closer to Him!

Remember the things that He has promised!

Remember who you are in Him!

He knows, He sees, He cares **_for you!!!!!_**

Forgive! Forgive yourself, forgive the ones who have harmed you, and accept God's forgiveness for yourself and others.

"And walk in love, just as Christ also loved you and gave Himself up for us" <u>Ephesians 5:2.</u>

Hippocratic Oath for Christians:

I swear to fulfill, to the best of my ability and judgment this covenant between myself and my God.

I will respect the hard-won victories that my Savior has won and the souls that He has saved.

I will gladly share such knowledge as is mine with those who are to follow.

I will apply all measures which are required to help each soul reach heaven.

I will remember that warmth, sympathy, and understanding may outweigh every word that I might say

I will not be ashamed to say "I don't know" nor will I fail to call in someone who might have the skills needed to help someone.

I will respect the privacy of those God entrusts me with, for their problems are not disclosed to me so that the world may know.

I will be especially careful in matters of life and death.

If it is given to me to save a soul then thanks be unto God. This great responsibility must be faced with humility and awareness of my own frailty. Above all I must not play God.

I will remember that I do not treat a symptom, but a human being.

I will prevent harm whenever possible, for prevention is preferable to a cure.

I will remember that I am part of the body of Christ; a special group of chosen souls that Jesus has claimed for His own.

May I always act so as to preserve the finest traditions of my calling as a Christian.

Pastor Derek Craig Jones

Pastor Derek Jones has been a minister of the Gospel for many years, beginning in his home church of Iron Mountain Assembly of God in Iron Mountain Missouri.

His calling is to make the Word of God understandable for everyone.

If you have any questions you can contact Pastor Jones at revdcj@yahoo.com or by mail at Pastor Derek Jones, PO Box 253, Desoto Mo. 63020

Made in the USA
Columbia, SC
25 August 2019